Cradle

of the

AMERICAN

Circus

Cradle
of the
AMERICAN
Circus

Poems from
Somers,
New York

Jo Pitkin

THE
History
PRESS

Published by The History Press
Charleston, SC 29403
www.historypress.net

First published 2012

Manufactured in the United States

ISBN 978.1.60949.637.1

Library of Congress CIP data applied for.

*For Florence "Mickey" Oliver
and the people of Somers*

Friday I tasted life. It was a vast morsel. A circus passed the house—I still feel the red in my mind...

—Emily Dickinson,
from a letter written to Mrs. J.G. Holland in 1866

Contents

CONTENTS

Preface

It all started with Samuel Whittemore. Nearly every day, I passed a stone monument in Arlington, Massachusetts, bearing this inscription:

> *Near this spot*
> *Samuel Whittemore,*
> *then 80 years old,*
> *killed three British soldiers*
> *April 19, 1775.*
> *He was shot, bayoneted,*
> *beaten and left for dead,*
> *but recovered and lived*
> *to be 98 years of age.*

After growing up in Somers, New York, I lived for decades just outside Boston, where history, especially Revolutionary War history, was palpable. I read historical plaques sprinkled on houses and streets, took note of statues in town greens and strolled through seventeenth- and eighteenth-century cemeteries on Copp's Hill or near King's Chapel. Every Patriot's Day in April, my adopted community celebrated local colonial heroes like Samuel Whittemore, who sought to break from oppressive British rule. During my daily travels doing ordinary things, I was constantly reminded of who had once lived in this place and what events had taken place here.

According to Mark Twain, "Distance lends enchantment to the view." In my case, this was true. Those numerous Bay State historical signs and monuments spurred me to consider my own hometown's history. Being in a place steeped in history made me curious about where I was from, my own local legacy. What did I really know about Somers?

I knew, of course, that an elephant loomed large in Somers history. My childhood was threaded with tales about Old Bet, the town's resident pachyderm. A third-grade teacher, Mary Egan, made sure all elementary school students knew the story of Old Bet and her owner, Hachaliah Bailey. A Somers native, Mrs. Egan famously collected elephants made out of glass, ceramic, wood and other materials. In 1966, my sister Barbara and I took part in a stirring "Stamp Day" parade, with papier-mâché and live elephants, for the purpose of celebrating Somers's official designation as "Cradle of the American Circus." At school, I cheered for the Tuskers—not the Cougars, the Lions or another sports team with a "normal" name. An elephant was emblazoned on our shiny fire trucks and one police car. Most importantly, a statue of an elephant held and still holds a watchful vigil in front of the town hall, which is called, well, the Elephant Hotel. Growing up in Somers, the significance of the elephant to our community was unavoidable. But was there more to the story?

In the 1990s, I decided to write a sequence of poems about my hometown's unusual history. I began researching the traveling menagerie and some of the Somers figures I had heard about through local lore. As my project took shape, I used whatever resources I could at the time to delve a bit deeper. What I uncovered was that other ordinary farmers and drovers besides Hachaliah Bailey had created, shaped and molded the traveling menagerie business in the early nineteenth century. I was amazed. I had no idea that—along with several *different* elephants besides Old Bet—lions, leopards, monkeys, hippos, giraffes, rhinos, ostriches, zebras, camels and other exotic animals had also lived, worked and died in Somers in the 1800s. I began to see my town differently.

How I researched the historical background for *Cradle of the American Circus* is a story in itself. Because I initiated this project before the advent of the Internet, information was not accessible at the click of a mouse. Instead, I tried to find and read accounts through the local library system. When relevant texts were not available, I attempted to purchase copies. In one case, I wrote a letter (no e-mail yet!) directly to circus historian Stuart Thayer and ordered both volumes of his self-published yet definitive *Annals of the American Circus*. I joined the Circus Historical Society so that I could read issues of its informative magazine, *Bandwagon*. To soak up atmosphere, I even attended a live performance of the Big Apple Circus when it toured Boston.

Immersing myself in historical materials certainly prepared me to write. When I had gone as far as I could as an independent researcher, I realized that I needed to be physically in Somers. I arranged a number of trips home to spend time in the archives housed at the Elephant Hotel, under town historian Florence Oliver's watchful eye. Working there during hours when the museum was closed, I had unlimited access to the exhibits, the circus library and the materials owned by the Somers Historical Society. I remember asking, "Do I have to wear protective white gloves?" because I was going to handle fragile, irreplaceable documents. I opened old metal filing cabinets crammed with fascinating material: hotel receipts, bills of sale, letters home, passports. It appeared that no one had looked in these files for a long, long time.

On one of my visits, I talked at length with Mrs. Oliver, peppering her with questions to which I had not been able to unearth satisfactory answers. As afternoon sun streamed in the tall, rounded windows on the third floor, I sat with her at a big table in the "library." She tried to answer my questions with facts and reasonable suppositions that stemmed from her own years of thoughtful research. The result of our conversation that afternoon was a poem full of questions: "In Search of History."

At the same time that I was looking into facts about traveling menageries, I read selected literary models that dealt with small-town American life or what I like to call "hamlet pride." These included volumes of poetry as well as works of prose: *Tilbury Town* by Edwin Arlington Robinson, *Spoon River Anthology* by Edgar Lee Masters, *Paterson* by William Carlos Williams, *The Country of the Pointed Firs* by Sarah Orne Jewett, *Main Street* by Sinclair Lewis, *Winesburg, Ohio* by Sherwood Anderson. Such works of literature provided me with inspiration and helped me figure out how best to tell the story I wanted to tell.

As I began writing the first poems about Somers in the early 1800s, a couple of patterns emerged. First, I decided that these poems would be largely dramatic monologues from the point of view of the showmen, the animals and other residents. Rather than re-creating the voices of dead citizens as Masters had done when he composed his masterpiece about the fictional Spoon River, I wanted my subjects to be people who were very much alive and thriving. Second, I had not forgotten Arlington's poor old Sam Whittemore entirely. Recognizing that the context for the poems would be obscure to most readers, I decided to include short prose passages. Interspersed among the poems, these concise passages would provide factual information to make the poetic content clearer. To my mind, these "prose plaques" would have the essence of a tour and would evoke the historical plaques I used to read in Arlington. It seemed to me that the end result—a hybrid work of literature— suited the singular subject matter well. Lastly, I realized that I would have to rely on my imagination to portray what the showmen, their families and their audiences might have been like. Although I used the historical record as a basis, I necessarily took great liberties in extrapolating individual personalities and motivations.

Another important aspect of the writing of *Cradle of the American Circus* was my significant change in attitude. At the beginning, I was set to dislike the exploitative businessmen who had made, figuratively, a killing by showing animals. The traveling menagerie had its critics in the nineteenth century, as I later discovered, but I was influenced by the prevailing attitudes of animal rights activists toward the circus in the late twentieth century. However, as I read historical materials and handled artifacts of the era, I began to find my own emotional connection to my town's former residents—and fell in love with them. They were inspiring, clever, adventurous, successful, inventive. What an improbable pursuit! What obstacles they had to overcome! It became clear to me that whatever I wrote about early showmen had to reclaim properly their "lost" history and to mirror the creativity that they demonstrated as they created, combined and adapted shows to keep their business ventures fresh and viable.

After years of working sporadically, I eventually completed this book-length sequence of poems about the unique history of my hometown. It is by no means comprehensive. There are more stories to tell, more poems to write. Yet *Cradle of the American Circus* does celebrate an extraordinary enterprise that was spawned by enterprising farmers and cattle drovers from Somers—and neighboring towns such as North Salem, Southeast, Carmel and Brewster. Its participants have infrequently received the credit they deserve for their many *firsts* in a distinct field of popular entertainment. Folks from my small corner of the world brought the first giraffes to America, first entered a lion's cage and created the first portable circus tent. In giving voice to some of these pioneering showmen, my aim is to highlight the significant role that Somers played in the evolution of the American circus while celebrating the underlying spirit that helped shape me.

Acknowledgements

"Cradle" was awarded Best Poem in the First Annual Hudson Valley Poetry Contest.

"Stone House" was a finalist in the 2006 Newburyport Art Association Poetry Contest judged by Erica Funkhouser and was published in *Riverine: An Anthology of Hudson Valley Writers*, edited by Laurence Carr (Codhill Press/SUNY Press, 2007).

"Farmers & Drovers" was published in the anthology *In the Black/In the Red: Poems of Profit & Loss*, edited by Gloria Vando and Philip Miller (Helicon Nine Editions, 2012).

"Route Book" appeared in CRAB ORCHARD REVIEW 17, no. 2, "Due North" issue.

"Cradle of the American Circus," "Elephant Hotel," "Gerard Crane" and "Roxanna Crane" appeared in *Henry: A Hudson Valley Journal of Creative Expression*, edited by Karen Ann Chaffee (Flamingo Publications, Spring 2011; www.flamingopublications.com).

The completion of this book was supported in part by the Massachusetts Arts Lottery, as administered by the Arlington Arts Council.

I wish to thank the late Florence S. Oliver, town historian of Somers; Terry Ariano, former town curator; and the Somers Historical Society for assistance in historical research.

I owe a debt of gratitude for the enthusiasm of Frank Billingsley, the unfailing insight and advice of Kate Whouley and the invaluable hands-on assistance and tireless guidance of Grace Zimmermann.

Thanks, too, to Mabel Addis, Frances Billingsley, Barbara Buchar, Mary Egan, Otto Koegel, Elizabeth Macauley, Jean Reidy, Kay Staplin and the numerous teachers and residents who have passed on their passion for the history of Somers to future generations.

I would also like to thank Bruce B. Anderson, Ann Greenberger, Lisa Moore, Marjie Polster, Gayle Roby and Zan Tewksbury for their manuscript suggestions and their enthusiastic support.

My thanks to The History Press, especially to Whitney Tarella for her persistence and creative vision and to Jaime Muehl for her keen editorial eye.

As always, I am deeply grateful to my parents, Margaret and Frank; to my sister, Barbara; and to Tom Alexander for their love and encouragement.

Introduction

CRADLE OF THE AMERICAN CIRCUS

By Florence "Mickey" Oliver

I am not going to talk about the circus personalities who slept in the cradle. I'm going to talk about the cradle itself—in other words, the community—that nurtured these personalities. In order to do that, let me take you back to the beginning of the nineteenth century, when Somers (or Stephen Town, as it was then called) was a thriving, growing community. The Croton Turnpike, organized in 1807 and running from Southeast to Sing Sing, joined with the road to Peekskill…just as the two roads do today. The Elephant Hotel had not yet been built, but there was a structure on the site, and the same year that the turnpike was organized, Hachaliah Bailey bought the property. Hachaliah's brother-in-law, Joshua Purdy, was the first director of the turnpike company, and two years later, the directors ordered that a gate be "erected on and across the said road on Somers Town Plane, near the house of Hachaliah Bailey." Smart cookies those Baileys and Purdys. Other directors and shareholders over the years will sound familiar to circus fans: Thaddeus Crane, Gerard Crane, John Titus, John J. June and Caleb S. Angevine.

So picture the hamlet in that first decade of the nineteenth century: a well-traveled road, with a toll gate at each end—one operated by Hachaliah Bailey, the other by Isaac Brown, the father of Benjamin and Christopher Brown. The road was flanked on both sides by shops of craftsmen and artisans; a lawyer; a doctor; a tavern or two; some general stores, selling everything from salt to ribbon; an academy; and, of course, a church. In 1809, Milton Cushing started a newspaper, one of the earliest in the county, and at about the same time Somers got its own post office.

The whole nation was in a period of rapid economic growth. Somers was part of that growth. It was still predominantly an agricultural economy but no longer the almost self-sufficient economy of the preceding generations. The men born during the Revolution now had cash crops (produce, wool, flax, etc.). They had money to spend and products with which to barter. The shops and stores that sprang up in the hamlet provided the goods and services they needed. Milton Cushing's newspaper, the *Somers Museum*, while published for only a very short period of time, and while it says nary a word about the appearance of an animal called an elephant on the village street, does, through its advertisements, give us an idea of the kinds of goods and services available in this growing community.

The Croton Turnpike and the road to Peekskill became important thoroughfares. Over them passed men on foot, on horseback and in wagons and carriages. Farmers got their produce to Sing Sing and Peekskill for shipment to New York City. Stagecoaches and mail coaches became common and exciting sights. Droves of cattle and sheep from one to three miles in length frequently wended their way through this hamlet.

The fattening of cattle had become a very important occupation in Somers. The practice was for the farmer to go to the counties to the north and west, buy up large herds of cattle, bring them here, fatten them on the farm and then drive them to New York City. It was, according to Culver, who wrote the chapter about Somers in *History of Westchester County*, edited by J. Thomas Scharf, a rare thing to find a farmer who was not also a drover. "It was in this way that many of the residents of the town laid the foundations of a large property." And eventually some of these farmers who had become drovers became menagerie owners and showmen.

They were hardy souls, these men. To be sure, they must also have had a bit of the wanderlust in them. They obviously were also

Masthead of the *Somers Museum and Westchester County Advertiser*, which was published weekly from 1809 to 1811 and cost $1.75 for a yearly subscription. Publisher Milton Foster Cushing (1787–1811) from Pawling, New York, died in an epidemic at the age of twenty-four, just two months before the birth of his son Stephen. *Courtesy of the collections of the Somers Historical Society.*

shrewd businessmen and managers—of both animals and people. The letters and documents in our archives show them to be literate, knowledgeable, intelligent men. The houses they built would indicate that they did very well in this "peculiar calling." Quoting from Scharf again, Culver states that "thousands of dollars were invested in these enterprises, and in many instances very profitable returns were realized." It seems strange to me that Culver doesn't say more about the circus, particularly since there must have been people around at the time (1886) who had been directly or indirectly involved. Were they perhaps reluctant to talk about it? Were their stories better left untold? Certainly this business must have had an impact on the community—in its values, its social life, its economy. Someone had to provide the meat and fodder for the animals. Did the local carriage maker make the circus wagons? Did Ezra Baxter, the tailor, make some elephant trappings? Did Noah Newman, the harness maker, get some business? How about Bailey Brown's saddler's shop? Did he perhaps make saddles for the performing horses? Were the tailor, the clock maker and Mr. Cushing himself competing with the lure of the circus when they advertised for apprentices? Did Mr. Cushing, who advertised that all kinds of job printing would be "elegantly executed," print any broadsides?

These circus men traveled as far west as the Mississippi River, to the Caribbean, to England and to Africa. Certainly they brought home new ideas, new fashions, sometimes even new wives. They also brought back money to invest and reinvest in real estate, pretentious homes, furnishings and other businesses unrelated to the circus and banking.

Hachaliah Bailey, when he built the Elephant Hotel (1820–1825), must have envisioned a long period of growth for his hometown. It is true that it may have been intended to become the meeting place for the menagerie owners. It was also intended to accommodate the travelers passing through a very busy community, the drovers and the merchants. Hachaliah did not have to submit an environmental impact statement to the town fathers. The townspeople must certainly, however, have been aware of what he had in mind. Do you suppose there was opposition to it—because of its size and bulk and the traffic it would generate? Or did they welcome it for the jobs it would create, both during its construction and afterward? The building did not go up overnight, and many local and itinerant artisans and laborers must have been employed. The bricks, Scharf tells us, were manufactured on the property. We now know exactly where the kiln was located—an IBM property across the road. The archaeologists hired by IBM to prepare a portion of the environmental impact statement definitively located it.

Shortly after the hotel was completed, Hachaliah had the statue to Old Bet carved and placed on a granite shaft in front of it. We don't know the name of the artist who took some blocks of white ash, glued them together and carved a replica of an elephant. We do know that Thaddeus Barlow, the local blacksmith, forged the ironwork to hold the statue. The granite shaft was hardly made by an amateur. Incidentally, the statue out there now is not the original. After a hundred years or so, it finally succumbed to bees and woodpeckers and had to be replaced...

The community continued to grow. In came a shoemaker, a cabinetmaker, a butcher, a hat factory, a millwright. At the center of it all stood the Elephant Hotel. It became the social, economic and political center not only of this community but also this whole area. And the circus fever had spread.

On January 14, 1835, 129 individuals and companies, all presumably involved in one way or another with this strange business, met at the Elephant Hotel and signed the Articles of Association of the Zoological Institute—it's long and very legal sounding. I wonder if perhaps Frederick J. Coffin, the attorney who lived across the street and advertised that "business in the professional line was attended to with fidelity," drafted the document. It begins by saying that the owners of the several menageries and exhibitions of wild animals and several caravan companies had united their interests in one joint company for the purpose of exhibiting the wild animals belonging to them for profit and that they had established an association to be known as the Zoological Institute, "which it is proposed to maintain for keeping a large collection of rare and curious animals, and exhibiting them…at such times and places, in such lots and parcels, and in such manner as shall best promote their interests; and by means of which the knowledge of natural history may be more generally diffused and promoted and rational curiosity gratified." To that end, they appraised the value of the several wild animals and other effects of the individuals and companies at $329,325. The directors were to keep transfer books, a record book, a minute book and account books. Where have all these books gone? They

Formed in 1835, the Zoological Institute absorbed all sixteen menageries in the United States, creating a monopoly. The number of menageries dropped to seven for the 1836 season. After the Panic of 1837, the organization failed, and its property was sold at auction on August 22 and 23. *Courtesy of the collections of the Somers Historical Society.*

St. Luke's Episcopal Church, Route 100, Somers, New York. *Photograph by Jeff Zimmerman.*

were also directed "to arrange and classify the animals belonging to the Association into different stationery [*sic*] exhibits and travelling caravans." The annual meetings for the election of directors were to be held at the Zoological Institute at No. 37 Bowery in New York City in December. In June and September, the board of directors was to meet at the Elephant Hotel in Somers "to exhibit...a detailed statement of the affairs and pecuniary concerns of the association

Stock certificate from the Farmers and Drovers Bank, which was founded in Somers in 1839 in the Elephant Hotel. *Courtesy of the collections of the Somers Historical Society.*

to the shareholders…present, and to pay dividends, if any." Leases for property in New York City held by Lewis B. Titus and Jesse Smith of North Salem and Gerard Crane and Thaddeus Crane of Somers were to be held by them in trust for the association. The life of the association was very short. The Panic of 1837 may have caused its breakup. It was not, however, the end of the world for the area menagerie and circus owners…

The circus was not, of course, the only concern of these men and this community. St. Luke's Episcopal Church (still standing on the other side of Bailey Park) was incorporated on January 26, 1835. The Episcopalians had been worshipping with the Presbyterians in the Old Union Meetinghouse for over thirty-five years. It's interesting to note that some of the men meeting to incorporate the new church had just twelve days earlier signed the Articles of Association of the Zoological Institute. Could it be that their exposure to the outside world had made them too worldly for the staid old Presbyterians?

Again, four years later, in 1839, some of these same men gathered together, again at the Elephant Hotel, and organized the Farmers and Drovers Bank of Somers—the second bank in all of Westchester County—at a time when the population of Somers was greater than either White Plains or Yonkers. Nearly half of the original shares of the bank were held by men who had some connections with the circus. Its first president was Horace Bailey, one of Hachaliah's cousins, who had purchased the hotel in 1837.

And so it went! That the circus had an impact on the community cannot be denied. The hotel and Old Bet's statue are the focal points of the town of Somers, reminding those of us who live here of our heritage and our unique place in the history of the circus.

CRADLE OF THE AMERICAN CIRCUS

PROLOGUE

From ochre burnt stones and crooked apple trees,
from swan-brimmed lakes and tart meadowfields,
from whiskey-colored barns and brick of hamlets,
from bleached bone buried scares in sudden woods
and tiger-striped lilybeds, come one, come all.

From forgotten paths and silences and eclipses,
from a ruined rhinoceros creek and runes of hay,
from water splashing, swinging scythes sweating,
from persimmon mingling with pasture and peat,
come threads of chance and glory, all come.

Come whispers, whistles, rustles in the grass.
Come clapboard glitter, crossroads sequins, midget calls.
Between scarred aisles of granite-stone cliffs, hear lions
in the maniacal roar of traffic, stranded owls in the lone
hoot of trains. Passing shadows. Wagons and tents.

Come salty air tasting of hides, cleanse our forests.
Come cheetahs and chimpanzees into tethered light.
From storehouses stuffed with grain and goldleaf,
from a cornucopia of clowns and ore and acrobats,
from dreaming riders and white horses, come all.

DR. HUGH GRANT ROWELL (1892–1963) from Tarrytown, New York, created this one-thousand-piece miniature circus model. The model, based on the traveling units of Barnum & Bailey and Ringling Brothers Circuses in the early 1900s, was exhibited at the opening of the film *The Greatest Show on Earth* at the Roxy Theater in 1952. Dr. Rowell's extensive collection of circus memorabilia was donated to the Somers Historical Society. Photograph by Jeff Zimmerman. Courtesy of the collections of the Somers Historical Society.

IN 1966, the United States Post Office Department issued a special cancellation giving Somers the official designation "Cradle of the American Circus." Somers boasts a memorial to Old Bet, America's second elephant, and the Elephant Hotel, which today houses a world-renowned circus museum. Some of the exhibited items include a suit worn by Tom Thumb when he appeared before England's Queen Victoria, a rhinoceros horn, a circus drum, Old Bet's trappings and other related ephemera.

CRADLE OF THE AMERICAN CIRCUS

Welcome to the cradle, the home base.
To your left find tusks, dried tiger skin,
a petrified elephant foot with its chain.
And there, a black velvet suit worn
by the famous midget 28 inches high.
From a curved window, to your right,
view the sentimental granite pedestal
with the bronzed elephant perched upon it,
ready for the big top one last time.
Angry farmers in Maine killed her,
the devil from Africa, with rakes and hoes.
Finally, if you look very carefully
into the 20th-century replica
of the 19th-century circus ring,
you'll see tiny lions jump through tiny hoops,
pink acrobats burn past like matchsticks,
apes and bears wear mock miniature fierceness.
This is where I live.
In the small House of Mirrors,
in the burning hoop.

Oil portrait of
HACHALIAH BAILEY,
artist unknown. Courtesy of
the collections of the Somers
Historical Society.

• •

HACHALIAH BAILEY (1775–1845) was a farmer, cattle drover, toll gate operator and hotel owner. Between 1804 and 1808, he purchased a four-year-old female African elephant for $1,000 and brought her from New York City to his home in Somers. Capitalizing on the public's fascination with Old Bet, he exhibited her throughout New York and New England and helped spark the menagerie craze that gripped residents of Somers and nearby towns in the early to mid-1800s. Bailey died in Somers from a horse's kick. His tombstone bears the inscription "Enterprise, Perseverance, Integrity."

HACHALIAH BAILEY

Enterprise

Here, talk floats like pipe smoke in air.
I drink my ale at the Bull's Head Tavern
in New York's Bowery and seize one stray
whiff of possibility offered by noisy sailors.

My farm in Stephentown sinks with stones.
So I buy this stumbling creature for a song.
She'll sure haul my weighted crop and more.
I'll ship her up the churning Hudson on my sloop.

This elephant is worth her weight in stares.
I revise my plan, switch gears, play neighbors' fears:
they know zero about animals of distant continents.
Betty's tusks and trunk yield rumor, gossip, cash.

Perseverance

From toll gates carving up a long turnpike,
to swollen cattle staggering to stockyards,
to stagecoach stops stretching to Sing Sing,
to my red brick hotel glittering with notables,
I work to live. I live to work.

I plow and plow and plow some more
in imagination's fertile ground. I don't quit.
Throughout the local countryside I tour.
First, I moved my fortune in the dark night,
and then I leased her to handlers for a price.

Even though Old Bet was shot and killed,
she left me rich enough to leave the state.
*"Go friend, to India. Find me more elephants.
Buy Columbus, Little Bett."* Despite murder,
theft, disappointment, and deceit, I keep on.

Integrity

For a man who merely trafficked in curiosity,
who tapped the need to see, to know, to hold,
I mined seventy years and set the stage for other
dreamers, doers, daring backyard performers.

I checked each contract written by the book.
I signed on the dotted line, kept promises,
sold animals with a clean bill of health,
paid my partners cash on the barrelhead.

I hold no regrets for trading my farmer's life
to be the first keeper of the rare and the wild.

This lithograph shows curious onlookers inspecting an ELEPHANT IN A FARMER'S BARNYARD similar to one Hachaliah Bailey might have had. Courtesy of the collections of the Somers Historical Society.

A handwritten BILL OF SALE dated December 9, 1809. Cyrus A. Cady and John E. Russell sold Nero, the Royal Tiger, along with his cage, to Somers showman Benjamin Lent for $1,000. Courtesy of the collections of the Somers Historical Society.

Nero, the Royal Tiger

At your sale to Lent for a decent sum,
you licked dried blood from ebony gums.
You bared ice-white razors, ivory rage.
Your heart now jumps against its cage,
wet flecks like falling clumps of snow
foam thick black bars above and below.
With a compulsive's repetitious steps,
you pace in inches even when you sleep,
wear down thick pads and nails on paws.
Do growls erupt from a scripted page?
Is this distress real or trained for show?

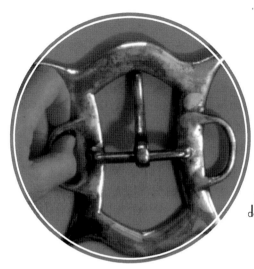

OLD BET is believed to have worn this belt buckle. It was donated to the Somers Historical Society by William Bailey, one of Hachaliah Bailey's descendants.

OLD BET, the second elephant brought to North America, was the star of Hachaliah Bailey's menagerie until her murder in Alfred, Maine, on July 24, 1816. An angry farmer named Donald Davis shot Old Bet, perhaps because he believed that she was an agent of the devil or because he felt it was sinful to spend hard-earned money on frivolous entertainment. Ten years after Old Bet's death, Bailey raised a monument to her—a wooden elephant painted gold and perched on top of wrought-iron scrollwork and a granite shaft—which still stands in front of the Elephant Hotel in the center of Somers.

OLD BET

Straw and gingerbread, potato peeling snacks.
Dream sandarac. Gray herds. Acacia trees.
Stiff golden trappings, gingerbread and straw.
Lumber, trumpet, kneel. Monotony of voices.
Clink chain, drink from bucket, riffle pockets.
Gingerbread and brocade trappings. Gold straw.
Strange buildings, frosty grass, bitter evergreen.
Sharp pine needles, heavy iron, bonfires in cold.
Kneel, lumber, trumpet. Potato peels. Iron prod.
Rough gold brocade. Midnight walk. Day parade.
Dog bark. Horse whinny. Pig snuffle. Wagon bray.
Lumber along dusty stone rough as heavy brocade.
Trumpet loud and sharp to stir stiff herds of voices.
Kneel on straw scented by potato skin, strange bread.

Albumen photograph of the ELEPHANT HOTEL, circa 1880, by an unknown photographer. Courtesy of the collections of the Somers Historical Society.

●●●

HACHALIAH BAILEY built the Elephant Hotel, a Federal-style red brick building, in 1825. Situated at a crossroads of the New York City–Albany and New York City–Boston routes on the Old Croton Turnpike, the hotel was a stop for Bailey's Eagle and Red Bird stagecoach lines and was frequented by cattle drovers, showmen, post riders and famous guests such as Horace Greeley, Aaron Burr and Washington Irving. In 1923–24, D.W. Griffith and his actors were headquartered here during the filming of *America*. The hotel has also served as a bank, tearoom, private residence, town hall and circus museum. It was dedicated as a National Historic Landmark in 2005.

ELEPHANT HOTEL

Imagine an architect's paradise,
how to solve the tough problems
of height and width and weight,
how to soundproof the beehive
of cramped rooms that will echo
with trumpeting blasts of rage,
whether showers are optional,
the logistical nightmare of trunks.

Then the decorator's dark humor:
ivory appointments, gray leather.

The vexed, jittery young innkeeper
with his heavy clank of keys paces
and prays that none of his visitors
will be rogue and wreck the place.

And the poor cook! One hundred
pounds of hay per guest per day!

Now, gleaming, white corridors
will one day be marked and marred
with nicks of tusks, granite stairs
will roll with years of heavy steps.

An 1839 oil portrait of GERARD CRANE by Ammi Phillips. Phillips (April 24, 1788– July 11, 1865) was an important itinerant American folk artist who was born in Colebrook, Connecticut. Courtesy of the collections of the Somers Historical Society.

GERARD CRANE (1791–1872) was a prosperous menagerie owner, town supervisor, director of the Farmers and Drovers Bank and vestryman of St. Luke's Episcopal Church. He first toured with a lion exhibit in 1818 and later purchased a rhinoceros, which he kept in a pen in a creek near his home. When the rhinoceros was being exhibited, an eight-horse team hauled it from town to town. Throughout his thirty-three-year career, Crane was variously affiliated with his brother Thaddeus and other successful showmen.

GERARD CRANE

How shiny are the buttons on my vest!
How deep the plush on my carriage seat!
I keep burnished chimpanzees in my barn;
my rhinoceros swims in Rhinoceros Creek!
I feel nearly Greek. I shall run for treasurer.
And I shall win. I shall collect and spend lavish coins
in the pockets and fissures of this town!
I shall shock the hamlet with schemes and profitable plans!
The roar of commerce will thunder from my land.
My sons and daughters will inherit a legacy of clowns.
Ministers will visit my monkeys! My wife will curry lions.
How rich the ring of chatter in my ample hip-roof barn!
How graceful the children ring-a-rosy dancing in silk!
How aromatic the crisp ones and fives. The rain. The trees I own!

The STONE HOUSE where Gerard and Roxanna Crane and their children lived is now listed on the National Register of Historic Places. In 1934, renowned American photographer Walker Evans (1903–1975) photographed both the Stone House and the Elephant Hotel. *Courtesy of the collections of the Somers Historical Society.*

GERARD CRANE and his wife, Roxanna, lived in Stone House, a Greek Revival mansion built in 1849 from native cut stone. Crane's home features a five-hundred-pound carved front door, carved marble mantels imported from Italy and elaborate plaster moldings and cornices. A hip-roof barn that once housed large menagerie animals stands on the property near what has become known as Rhinoceros Creek. Walker Evans, who always kept notes on his subjects and had a habit of making several versions of each picture to experiment with slightly different combinations of images, photographed Stone House in the fall of 1934.

STONE HOUSE

From a 1934 Walker Evans Photograph of the Crane Home, Somers, New York

In the foreground, a few silvered strips of fence. The
yard's topiary made from light. I see a gravel path like
a brush of yellow dust. Monument. In the center,
shadows move on granite like dark moss, and dark ivy
mosses stone. An iron fence of spikes gates the wild.
Pastoral brush. Twin giant pines shine tinseled by
hanging heavy cones. As November sun spills
silvered coins over dark moss shadows and stark cones
of pillars, a tinsel stain darkens light granite. Twin
chimneys fence off the background. Now the focus is
the iron-stained door, from which, all at once, a man
in a gravel-colored suit, perhaps smoking the hollow
cone of a cigar or cradling a rolled paper, may appear.
The hidden conversation between rooftop, tree
branch, sky.

An 1839 portrait of ROXANNA PURDY CRANE by Ammi Phillips, oil on canvas. Courtesy of the collections of the Somers Historical Society.

ROXANNA CRANE

As I draw a steely metal comb
through one monkey's rusted fur,
I teethe out dry gnats, gnarls, fleas.
How I covet simple tasks: sewing,
baking, bleaching, washing, ironing!

I shut and lock my bedroom doors.
I jerk the garish, jewel-studded collar
off my little pawn's reddish head.
I draw down layers of snowy lace
from my swollen chin to my cold throat.

Peeping out frosted, imported panes
with the silence of a master mime,
I test then inch by inch by inch wrap
the warm, puckered, glittering strap
around my pulsing plain white neck.

In the early 1800s, the distinctive STONE HOUSE BARN, located on Route 202 and owned by Gerard Crane, housed menagerie animals during the winter seasons. Near the barn runs a small stream known as Rhinoceros Creek, where Crane's rhinoceros was often kept. One summer, the rhino did not go out on tour but was instead placed in a pen built in the brook's deep ravine. According to local legend, the rhino knocked down one end of its pen and walked into town. Imagine seeing that! *Courtesy of the collections of the Somers Historical Society.*

RHINOCEROS CREEK

Ice like old skin or mottled hide of blue,

    seal inside those secret wishes,

        hold back a wellspring, keep in silence

           what worlds in winter you cover over.

       In spring, after rain, crack and wrinkle,

    shed only a little wet grief at night

in the speckled moonlight flashing.

      Now, writhing, desperate escapee,

        let pass a distant herd drumming and roaring,

           free gray streams of water folding over

        round rocks and green eelgrass unraveling like
           unpinned hair,

pause at the still, pooled navel in the center of flowing, rushing,
    hushing air.

      Then, by day, greet the barrier of sedge and stone

        with sudden profusion, an understanding.

The home of
THADDEUS CRANE,
located at the corner of
Dean's Bridge Road and
Old Croton Falls Road.
*Courtesy of the collections of
the Somers Historical Society.*

• •

WITH HIS YOUNGER BROTHER GERARD, Thaddeus Crane purchased two Brazilian tigers, two African leopards, a coatimundi, two monkeys, two English organs, a bass drum, Italian cymbals, two circus wagons and five horses for $3,500. In 1825, he and his brother paid $3,000 to Marcus Sloat of Carmel for one-third interest in an elephant named Pet. Thad Crane, who died in 1849, is buried in Ivandell Cemetery alongside numerous fellow showmen and several generations of his namesakes.

THADDEUS CRANE

My sons and their sons and their sons—
glutted with dividends, shares, holdings—
do not have the means to cherish this
(mine and Uncle Gerry's) peculiar calling.

Although my name will be recarved
not once, not twice, but five times over,
these namesakes will never find gated here
among the Quicks, the Lents, the Browns
my raccoon-like coatimundi, my fire-yellow
tiger, my fine horses belled and kicking.

No, these I buried whisperingly
one at a time over the years at night alone
behind my spread on Dean's Bridge Road,
my bone-white forearms planted in mud.
Here, my true wealth is still ever secretly
squandered by rain, time, grief, shadow.

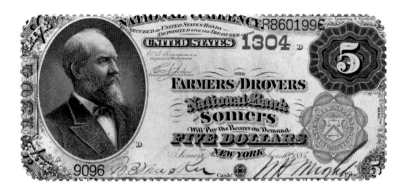

A FARMERS AND DROVERS BANK five-dollar note, 1885. The Farmers and Drovers Bank (1839–1885) was established in the Elephant Hotel in 1839 with menagerie money. Organized by Hachaliah Bailey's cousin Horace, this was the second bank in Westchester County. Courtesy of the collections of the Somers Historical Society.

IN THE EARLY 1800S, some Somers farmers became successful drovers. They traveled hundreds of miles to buy large herds of cattle and sheep and then drove them back to Somers, where the animals were fattened until they were ready to be driven to New York City stockyards. Applying their skills in doing business and handling animals, some drovers in turn became showmen in the fledgling yet lucrative traveling menagerie business. Hachaliah Bailey, himself a drover, reputedly acquired his elephant at the Bull's Head Tavern on New York City's Bowery, where drovers, cattle dealers and ship captains gathered to make deals, exchange news and enjoy exhibits of trained monkeys, bears and dogs.

Farmers & Drovers

Before my wet fields had shed their sleep,
my stoned-off pastures ripened with sheep.

Even rain didn't stop the endless work:
tend, raise, water, feed, drive, yoke.

I once had luck with apples and grain.
I switched to livestock until the trains

hauled heavy cattle miles to the city.
Now my fingernails are hardly dirty.

I buy and sell hyenas, zebras, gnus.
Llamas, polar bears, camels, emus!

Leopards, kangaroos, baboons, apes!
With this new livelihood, I can escape.

I still fill troughs, make beds of hay.
But now my wife and children stay

home while I travel the tillable world.
Around me, the fashions of cities swirl.

Each bill of sale is like a seed.
And green money grows like weeds.

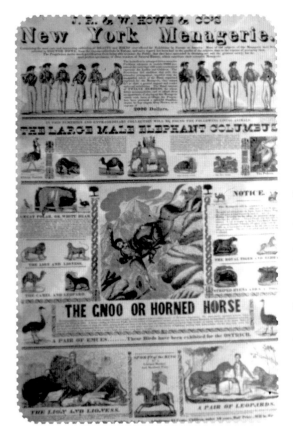

A J.R. & W. HOWE & CO. 1834 broadside advertising the New York Menagerie. The menagerie's owners, J.R. and William Howe Jr., hailed from North Salem, New York. Courtesy of the collections of the Somers Historical Society.

IN THE HEYDAY of the traveling menagerie from the early to mid-1800s, large audiences paid a quarter to view a variety of animals imported from Asia, Africa, Europe and the Caribbean. Part of the 1834 year-end inventory list of forty-two animals owned by the J.R. & W. Howe & Co. exhibition, then worth more than $46,000, appears in the next poem. From April to November, the traveling menagerie toured small towns and then combined with other menageries and circuses for the winter season, exhibiting animals in permanent arenas located in larger cities.

The Menagerie

Tangible science triumphs.
        Fear and rage are tamed.
                1 rhinoceros
                1 Elephant Columbus
Proof of God's existence,
        evidence of man's bit part,
snorts in makeshift crates.
                1 zebra
                1 Bactrian camel
                2 dromedaries
                1 gnoo
From unfamiliar worlds,
        twitch nature's aristocrats,
the kin of dogs and cats.
                2 Royal tigers
                4 leopards
                1 wild cat
New jobs are created!
        Handlers use drovers' skills.
Procurers scout deserts.
                1 spotted hyena
                1 White Bear
                1 Black do
From town to town to town,
        money changes hands.
                1 Riding monkey
                2 baboons
                11 cage monkeys

As John James Audubon
      killed and painted America's birds
a living aviary was opening—
              1 ostrich
              2 emews
              1 Cassawara
      cawing, scratching, flapping, preening—
              1 Pelican
              1 King of Vultures
              1 eagle
missing its swift silk triangle of flight,
              1 macaw
              1 cockatoo
              2 parrots
the rhythm of air, night hunting, rain.

Alive and lit by lanterns,
      the heavy ark rolls forward.

Rara Avis

How the prized white peacock
with its opening fan of snow,
of pearl, of oyster, of cameo
or the treasured black swan
with its huge jet wing spread
like a giant dark leaf bobbing
near the black banks of mud
would not have been a match
for the owl my father spotted
for us by day in the tall pine,
for one white swan or heron
who flew overhead this spring
from cemetery to reservoir
rustling the sky's dry cattails,
for thrushes and meadowlarks
performing a daily concert
to make these blooming hills
pulse with their hidden music.

The pianoforte that ALFRED COPS gave as a wedding present to his daughter Mary and her husband, Benjamin Brown. Donated by Mrs. Giles Whiting. Photograph by Richard Farmer Hess. Courtesy of the collections of the Somers Historical Society.

SOMERS NATIVE BENJAMIN BROWN (1799–1881) had his own circus and often toured with his brothers Christopher and Herschel or his cousins J. Purdy and Oscar Brown. In 1828, Brown's circus and Charles Wright's menagerie toured in the first traveling combination of a circus and menagerie. In 1838, Brown traveled to Egypt to purchase camelopards, or giraffes, for North Salem's June, Titus and Angevine. In 1840, Brown brought the giraffes to the United States and that same year exhibited them in London, where he met and married Mary Cops, daughter of the Tower of London's keeper of the royal menagerie.

BENJAMIN BROWN

In my youth, escaped from pirates.
Survived a forty-four-day fever.
Herded giraffes and their calves,
Noah-like, over 300 miles at night
in a scorching, scorpion-full desert.
Trekked to dark unmapped corners.
Shook hands with smiling cannibals.
Ate gazelle meat. Navigated the Nile.
Beat David Livingstone to the Kalahari.

Now, while listening to Mary's pianoforte
or clipping some of our garden's flowers,
I reminisce all alone. Ache-in-bones.
Finally, I can stop awhile to savor
the delirium of blowing fruit trees
in our yard's small green oasis.

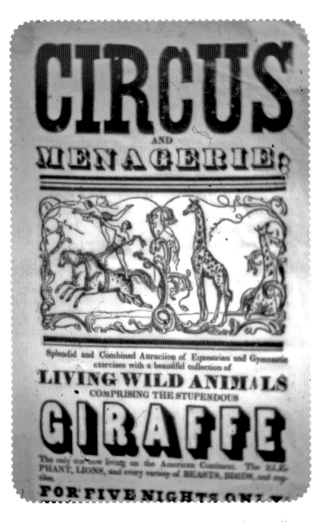

A CIRCUS AND MENAGERIE POSTER with a giraffe.
Courtesy of the collections of the Somers Historical Society.

THE CAMELOPARD

Tottering on four
stilt-saplings into
miniature towns,
she briefly rises
above the elegy
of native trees.
She must depend
on different men,
men whose jerk
can fatally snap
her pearly strand
of seven neck bones.
A novelty, she lives
only for the span
of a pause, a lapse,
for the diminished
tenure of the rare,
of the fragile,
of the once loved.

SAFARI

In day's glazed heat
that kindles like a brush
fire, the quiet interplay of small
and mammoth, muted gray and gaudy
neon, hunter and hunted at the edge of
a spreading, golden savanna. Here's a pageant
no one can create or sell. A cheetah pads
softly out of my shadow! And bearded gnus
stream across a marbled continent
like a river that constantly flows,
like the lymphatic Hudson River
that flows in me, from me.

ELEGY

They were packed like gold bars in a box.
They were loaded onto moaning ships.
Some died in airless holds. Some wanted to.

And here they are. Men with money and plans
bid and buy and sell—
        then it's the locked cage.

If they breathe heavily,
their thin ribs touch the sides.

They'll never again smell Africa.
The savanna is memory, dream.
        What is that sound? Cold?

Alone at night, they are left
with the jagged black stone
of a moment in which they lost

their mothers, their range, their flat-
top trees, their rain, their purple kills.

The clock of exile slowly moves.
Even death's poison, mold, stones,
        worms, or pale microscopic cells
do not return, renew, restore.

At night, they are left all alone
with their shit, scabies, acrid straw.

Following OLD BET's death, Hachaliah Bailey bought two more elephants, Little Bett and Columbus. Columbus died in March 1829 at the age of twenty-six. This picture appeared in an 1817 notice from the *Columbian Centinel*, a Boston newspaper, advertising Columbus's exhibition. *Courtesy of the collections of the Somers Historical Society.*

• •

AN ELEPHANT LAUNCHED the menagerie business and is still the icon of the modern circus. Captain Jacob Crowninshield brought the first elephant from India to the United States in 1796. Unlike other menagerie animals, elephants were able to survive for many years in captivity; however, a number of them met violent deaths. Like Old Bet, Little Bett was shot. Both Juliet and Columbus fell through bridges. Queen Anne died from drinking a barrel of ice water, Jumbo was hit by a train and Romeo died "from an overdose of pitchfork." If elephants experienced *musth*, an emotional state caused by periodic activity of the temporal gland, they often went on deadly rampages and were consequently destroyed.

ELEPHANT TRIPTYCH

One

From Crowninshield's nameless one
their American lineage artificially grew
in this humbled foreign space: Old Bet,
Columbus, Tippoo Sultan, Virginius, Juliet,
Romeo, Siam, Hannibal, Horatio, Little Bett,
Queen Anne, Bolivar, Pizarro, the notable Jumbo.

Transplanted, they hauled with them the long memory
of Hannibal crossing the deepsnow Alps,
of red paintings of woolly mammoths in red caves,
of Buddha's last white elephant incarnation.

Two

Cousin of clouds,
        flapping flags of ears,
                white-yellow ivory of tusks,
                        heavy logs of limbs—

        you're larger than the ionosphere.

Only a thousand bullets can stop you.

Or the swallowed bitter bloom
of cyanide secreted by a trusted friend
inside an apple or an orange's pitted rind.

Three

Before Darwin studied nature, naturalists
praised an elephant's *human* traits: loyalty,
docility, dignity, respectability, and restraint.

It's true. They live in families, make and use
simple tools, pass on what they know to offspring,
engage in war, work, die on average at sixty-five.

And, too, they can either tear down trees
or pick up a shiny coin with their proboscis,
that many-muscled, gray fog, fingered "hand."

Most adult males live in relative isolation.
They join families, close-knit herds of females,
for a short while just when they decide to mate.

They're so like us. They play, cry, fight, sulk, drink.
They become moody, unpredictable, or violent
when periodic *musth* stains their cheeks with black tears.

As they lumber past the fragile stumps of their domain,
they seem invincible. Yet at the waterhole, in woodlands,
in deserts, in grasslands, in rainforests, in salty caves,

they do not abuse the hyperbole of their weight and size.

WINTERING

Huddled in hothouse
barns in fields turned
arctic under the whip
of the wailing wind
or fed sallow strands
of weeds and stalks
in stocked cellars,
stalled menageries
idly snarl and squawk.
In the religious silence
of lightly falling snow,
stirs a restless promise:
sun, mud, the show.

A Bowery Amphitheatre
1840 broadside advertising a circus performance at the Zoological Institute's venue at 37 The Bowery in New York City. Courtesy of the collections of the Somers Historical Society.

• •

In the early days of the menagerie business, animals were housed for the winter season in country barns and cellars and cared for by farmers, menagerie owners and stockholders. Later, the Zoological Institute established permanent headquarters at 37 The Bowery, where animals from different menageries were kept and shown indoors in winter in a performance space that stretched across four city lots. The name of this structure was changed to The Bowery Amphitheatre after a stage and circus ring were added. This venue proved to be more popular than New York City theaters offering "legitimate" drama.

37 THE BOWERY

Where the wanderers came to rest,
Where the wealth of tired species
Paced away chill winter seasons,
Where the intimate give-and-take
Of voyeur and object of scrutiny
Was performed in dimmed corridors,
Where enlightened New Yorkers
Lost their nerve or found their faith,
Where a few moral citizens who paid
To pray, to shine their unwavering light
(Come into the light, come into the light)
And expose the howling spirit
Of unspeakable darkness housed there,
Stayed unexpectedly. Entranced.

MENAGERIE ADMISSION TICKETS. *Courtesy of the collections of the Somers Historical Society.*

•••

MENAGERIE ANIMALS WERE kept in small barred boxes called shifting dens. They were moved by wagon at night to prevent free shows. In the daytime, from noon to four o'clock, audiences paid a quarter to view animals in cages that were arranged on sawhorses around the wall of a tent or to watch simple ring performances by trained monkeys and elephants. Because menagerie animals were costly to import and keep and because the public began to grow tired of the same displays year after year, the traveling menagerie eventually combined with the circus.

THE WITNESS

Saw something oyster colored ripple
the bushes, part the steaming waters.

Not goat, not deer, not ram was it.
No cat. No badger. No cow. No ox.

Had a knobbed snout and hooves,
wore its skin like a lizard, bobbed

like a mute swan, brayed like a mule,
smelled rank, was square like a box.

Saw something. Quick. Then fog lifted
off like sulfur smoke from a lit match.

Knew my own self to be so small.
Held my breath tight in the dark.

Oh, take me, this lost, dazed child.
Show me. More. More, and more.

Georges Seurat, *LE CIRQUE* (The Circus), 1890–91. Oil on canvas, 185.5 x 152.5 cm. Musée d'Orsay, Paris. Erich Lessing/Art Resource, New York.

LE CIRQUE

From Georges Seurat's Last, Unfinished Painting

The smirking yellow trick rider flutters by,
a lithe canary or golden butterfly perched
on the bare back of a frightened white horse.
Above her, a drunken trio of fiddlers plays.
Acrobats tumble and twirl like windswept leaves.

Only the heavy navy blue sky is the limit.
Nothing inside the big red ring will stop them—
the gliding, swooping, springing, rolling acts—
from jumping higher, laughing more lewdly,
galloping faster, or somersaulting forever.

There, see, the impeccable ringmaster beams.
His thin, trimmed mustache is a taut black whip.
In black and white, he tries to keep a low profile.
From his corner, he counts heads and eyes *artistes*.
He's the elegant impresario of daring and dazzle.

Who are those polite men and women who stare
straight ahead, anchored to their hard rowed seats,
wearing derbies, bonnets, and caps on fixed heads?
They do not grin or flinch as this concentrated world
spins dizzyingly before them in flashing colors, joyous.

Addition to the GRAND CARAVAN, a poster advertising the Wright Brothers' menagerie. Courtesy of the collections of the Somers Historical Society.

EARLY TRAVELING MENAGERIES were advertised by word of mouth. As the traveling menagerie business grew, shows were advertised by means of newspaper ads in addition to handbills, posters and broadsides that were posted by an agent in local inns, stables and coach stations a week or so in advance of the show's arrival. Characterized by hyperbole, exclamation and colorful description, most menagerie advertising included lists of specific acts, performers and animals, as well as dates, times and admission prices. The first color poster, which promoted R. Sands and Company Hippoferaean Arena, was used in 1849.

Circus Poster

Rise up, black ostrich, out from your weeds!
Jaguar, jump out of your lair, your burrow!
In the trumpeting wind and drumming rain,
tattered bills printed in black newspaper ink
or bright dyes—cardinal, salmon, fawn, sable,
carmine, coral—promote the finest, the best,
the first, the biggest, the greatest, the only!
Tacked in taverns, coach stations, or stables,
these moveable billboards again and again
herald snow leopards, emus, and tigresses
whose human faces falsely grin and frown.
They leap out of unfamiliar deserts, moors!
The lean, suited men beside them are either
very small or train the largest of their type.
Standing in throngs, a hungry public drinks
in faded broadsides weathered like a fresco
or Albert Pinkham Ryder's temporary art,
knowing that they will be forever changed.
They want to be changed! They are changed!

A Brown & Co. CIRCUS BROADSIDE, circa 1836. J. Purdy Brown and Lewis Bailey teamed up as partners in a circus that Oscar Brown took over after his brother's death in 1834. Courtesy of the collections of the Somers Historical Society.

● ●

JOSHUA PURDY BROWN (1802?–1834) raised the first circus tent in November 1825 when his and cousin Lewis Bailey's circus appeared in Wilmington, Delaware. Brown devised a portable sailcloth tent that could be used in place of the traditional permanent wooden arena. His innovation allowed shows to go on despite foul weather and to travel more easily to more small towns. Brown was also the first manager to tour the United States with a combined menagerie and circus under a single ownership. He died in Mobile, Alabama, after eating poisoned crab.

J. Purdy Brown

My twisty knot of worries pricks me awake.
From my back to my stomach to my side,
I twist and turn. Against night's sleek panes
tinkles a dull shower of tarnished coins.
I'll have to cancel yet another show.

Then up snap opened umbrellas,
tan mushrooms in a fungal wood,
inverted tornado funnels, black clouds.
Rain stops. At last, the whole sweet night
lies comforted under its dense canopy of stars.

Sleep's thick cloth shade blots out the ruined day.

A ZOOLOGICAL INSTITUTE certificate for 120 stock shares dated February 21, 1833, to Charles Wright. Courtesy of the collections of the Somers Historical Society.

• •

ON JANUARY 14, 1835, a group of 128 showmen met at the Elephant Hotel to combine nine established menageries and form a joint-stock company called the Zoological Institute. Their mission was to exhibit "a large collection of rare and curious animals…by means of which natural history may be more generally diffused and promoted and rational curiosity gratified." Under the direction of a board of directors, the company sold stock, sought investors, assigned managers to shows, managed associated menageries' property, determined non-conflicting routes and classified animals in stationary or traveling exhibits. The institute, worth $329,325 when it was formed, dissolved after it failed during a financial collapse, the Panic of 1837.

THE ZOOLOGICAL INSTITUTE

Study royal tigers, jaguars, jackals.
Don't learn their Latin names,
genus plus specific epithet pinning
down their colors, homes, or finders.
Don't read Baron Georges Cuvier,
Lamarck, *Natural History* by Buffon.

Stand inside a room, barn, or tent.
Eye the never-before-seen cargo
sought and bought by neighbors,
unschooled American naturalists
who merge and split stock shares
in hyenas, zebras, polar bears.

Hold out a trembling hand. Touch.
Thumb dewlap and antler velvet.
Finger a peacock's jeweled-eye tail.
Paw spotted hide of flickering light.
Seek the violet ostrich swimming
in its cloudy, inviolable oval egg.

Witness enemies who once warred
at the darkening riverbank
now gather together in twilight
where the possible breathes.

A Morse, M'Kenney & Company 1856 COLOR WOODCUT advertising Sands, Nathans & Co. Circus. Richard Sands, a "ceiling walker," and his partner, equestrian John J. Nathans, belonged to the second generation of Flatfoots. Prints & Photographs Division, Library of Congress, LC-USZCN4-113.

● ●

THE FLATFOOT PARTY, like the Zoological Institute, was a powerful syndicate of showmen. The first generation of Flatfoots included North Salem's John J. June, Lewis B. Titus, Caleb S. Angevine and Jesse Smith and Somers's Thaddeus and Gerard Crane. Among the second generation were C.G. Quick, Richard Sands, George F. Bailey and Lewis June. The Flatfoots were an influential presence in the menagerie business from about 1838 to 1881. Their nickname apparently resulted from an adamant response to rival Raymond & Waring's planned summer tour of New York: "We put our foot down flat and shall play New York, so watch out."

THE FLATFOOTS

We import, sell, and lease beasts
from Asia, Africa, South America.
We manage, control, and promote
menageries with our own names
or front the cash to foot the bills
of shows put on by other men.

We buy in, sell out, loan, and deal,
capitalize on Darwin's infinite supply.
We synchronize routes west and east,
monopolize for more than fifty years,
invest in curiosity's growth potential,
merge money, dreams, farmers' savvy.

We drive a collective stake in the heart
of this new industry in this new territory.
We check an upstart rival's summer tour
to claim our New York state exclusively.
We put our foot down flat and take
the main chance, whatever it might be.

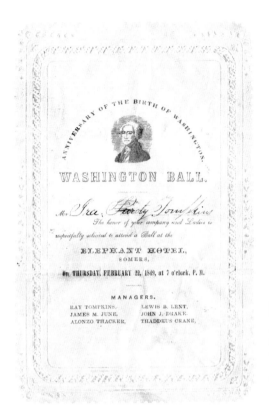

An invitation to the
WASHINGTON BALL
held on February 22,
1849. Courtesy of the
collections of the Somers
Historical Society.

●●●

THE GREAT SHOWMAN'S BALL was held on February 22, 1849, at the Elephant Hotel to celebrate the anniversary of George Washington's birth. Because the hotel could not accommodate the eight hundred showmen and local debutantes who attended the ball, guests were shuttled in shifts between the banquet hall and ballroom until 7:00 a.m. According to a newspaper account, the showmen, whose combined fortunes exceeded $5 million, were "hopeless Bachelors of the deplorable age of 45 and upwards, who although rich as grand Turks, set more value on a trained horse or elephant, than the attractions of lovely women."

THE GREAT SHOWMAN'S BALL

A knot of rich bachelors laughs and smokes
in the sequined corners of a mobbed hotel.
These chortling misers pinch their wealth
in wild creatures and keep safe in the shows
that mean more to them than any wife.
Glittering young gems who just sleighed in
from all over the county wait, wait, wait
for a once-in-a-lifetime reel or promenade.
They do not yet know that love will flare
and fade like white stars they cannot hold.
On this winter night, the ballroom blazes.
Shifts of blushing girls in gowns parade,
resigned to tonight's stark transactions
taking place on the springy dance floor.
They have been carefully trained to vie
for the gilt cage. To bid for the tame life.

LEWIS B. LENT, the son of Benjamin Lent, managed the New York Circus, which performed at the Hippotheatron on Fourteenth Street in New York City. Courtesy of the collections of the Somers Historical Society.

• •

IN THE 1830S, the distinction between two independent forms of entertainment—menagerie and circus—gradually began to blur. Traditionally, the circus had acrobats, clowns and equestrians; the traveling menagerie featured animals but no human performers. Little by little, circuses added a few wild animals, and menageries included bands of musicians and offered clown or equestrian acts for variety. Generally, women were not directly involved with early traveling menageries, with the exception of a handful of female animal trainers from 1848 on; however, equestriennes had been performing with American circuses since the late 1700s. Rosaline Stickney debuted in 1836 with Oscar Brown & Company, a circus that was owned by J. Purdy Brown's brother, and Southeast's Lily Forepaugh, who married the son of showman Adam Forepaugh, was a popular equestrienne of the late 1800s.

EQUESTRIENNE

I hear the joined *O*'s meaning *don't fall don't fall.* I
star the stage with life and death. Bright falling stars
attract less gaze than my bareback somersault. I attract
small gasps by dazzling audiences with skill and small
red sequins that shimmer like garnets. Those posters read
How she rides as fast as light or wind in storms! How
free these twirls and spins and leaps over banners freed
in a ring that holds the world in place. For a finale, in
faint pirouettes I dare the very air until a woman faints.
Horse, juggling rider, wooden ring blur to one. Hoarse
cheers unfurl, a canter slows to easy walk, lamps cheer
coming night as the spinning gyroscope stops. Come in
now, groom. Take my whip. Snuff flaming hoops. Now
rein my gentle white Chaos. Hear soft applause like rain.

Detail from the AMERICAN MENAGERIE poster, 1828, showing Charles Wright in a lion's cage. Courtesy of the collections of the Somers Historical Society.

SOMERS'S INNKEEPER MICAJAH WRIGHT'S three sons—Daniel (1790–1864), Charles (1792–1862) and James (1799–1864)—all became showmen. Daniel traveled with a menagerie and later settled in Ohio, and James toured with his brother Charles and J. Purdy Brown until settling in South Carolina and Alabama. Charles began his career exhibiting Little Bett, the third elephant brought to the United States, for Finch & Bailey. He later became the first American "Keeper of the Lions" for Carley, Purdy & Wright's Menagerie in 1830 and was the first American showman to enter a lion's cage.

CHARLES WRIGHT

Now James raises cotton
as Spanish moss, a canopy
of gray-green anacondas,
coils over his plantation.
And Daniel, after traveling
west with a show, settles
below Ohio's flattening horizon.

On my wedding day, I vow
to stay at home. Never wander.
Married to Elizabeth Maria Smith,
I'll run my modest farm
(but in the dark silently arrange
by letter routes and sales
in a calling I won't give up).

Who can stop
the first American man
to enter the flimsy cages
of hyenas, leopards, tigers, lions?

"First Sketch" by Eleanor Hollis Murdock Beach, 1947. Beach (1887–1965) and her husband, Chester (1881–1956), an accomplished sculptor, resided on a Starr Ridge Road estate in Brewster. Their red barn, built by James Bailey, housed menagerie animals in the winter. (James, the adopted son of Hachaliah's nephew Frederick, later partnered with P.T. Barnum in 1888.) Unfortunately, this barn was destroyed by fire in 1911. *Courtesy of Grace Zimmermann.*

• •

THE ZEBRA WAS among the many varieties of documented traveling menagerie animals. Somers native Charles Wright advertised a zebra in his collection in 1826. Wright's "New Caravan of Living Animals" also featured emus, a camel and monkeys. Although the modern zebra is associated with African wildlife, it is believed that its ancestor crossed the Bering land bridge from North America to Africa.

THE ZEBRA

Wearing your geometric coat of light

and the absence of light,

run and run in this green open place.

Kick and gallop in fenced

pastures far from the ancient land bridge

you once crossed in herds

east to west above vast, underground plates

shifting, moving, changing

our paths, our pasts, our common histories.

In pastoral flickering shade,

graze, snort, bark, sniff, shudder unafraid,

returned home, at last, by water.

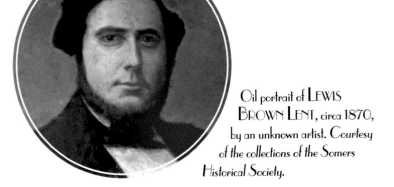

Oil portrait of LEWIS BROWN LENT, circa 1870, by an unknown artist. Courtesy of the collections of the Somers Historical Society.

LEWIS BROWN LENT (1813–1887) was the son of Somers showman Benjamin Lent. At the age of twenty-one, he became an agent for June, Titus and Angevine and acquired an interest in J.R. and W. Howe's Menagerie. From 1835 to 1837, Lent and Oscar W. Brown were partners in a circus. From 1857 until he retired in 1882, Lent acted as either an owner or manager of numerous shows, gaining himself a reputation as one of the foremost second-generation showmen. His own show, L.B. Lent's New York Circus, in 1866 became the first successful railroad circus. Lent is also credited with pioneering the use of "jaw-breaking" hyperbolic phrases to attract audiences.

LEWIS BROWN LENT

Was I the greatest agent of my day?
I could turn a profit, move shows smoothly,
make smart deals, invest shrewdly.

At home, my wife does the talking.
On paper, I find my voice:

Hemispheric Hippozoonomadon
Arenic marvels
Equescurriculum
Colossal quadrapedal company

When I'm all out and over, carry me home
in a horse-drawn ultramarine blue wagon.

Let there be white peacocks, a brass band.

A long, glittering, cosmographic caravan.

GEORGE F. BAILEY'S bandwagon with the band traveling on Broadway in Kilbourn City in the Wisconsin Dells. This photograph was taken by H.H. Bennett in June 1868. *Wisconsin Historical Society Image ID WHi-7756.*

NORTH SALEM'S GEORGE FOX BAILEY (1818–1903) was Hachaliah Bailey's nephew and veteran showman Aaron Turner's son-in-law. Bailey inherited Turner's circus and toured with it during the Civil War. After the war, Bailey joined the second generation of Flatfoots, including Richard Sands, J.J. Nathans and Avery Smith. In 1875, he helped the syndicate buy the financially shaky P.T. Barnum's Show, turned it around and sold it in 1880. Bailey, who invented the first traveling water tank to transport a hippopotamus around the country, was the last of the Flatfoots to die.

GEORGE F. BAILEY

I'm the lonely, sinuous trickle
of a drought-dried stream.
I'm the tolling bell of night.
I'm a flying caret of geese
just before winter's onset,
one shivering acorn on an oak,
one walnut-colored apple left
in a leafless brown orchard.

In evening's swirling smoke
and pink dust, I quietly perch
vulturelike on my porch.
With a spotted, papery claw,
I wave to blurry passersby
I may or may not know.
In the twilight, I connect
faint stars in constellations.

Each arbitrary link reminds me
of the lost spidery branches
of someone's dying family tree.

A lithograph of the GEORGE F. BAILEY HIPPOPOTAMUS.
When Bailey's circus arrived in Amherst, Massachusetts, on
Friday, May 4, 1866, Emily Dickinson wrote a letter to Elizabeth
Holland about watching the procession make its way past her house.
Courtesy of the collections of the Somers Historical Society.

THE HIPPOPOTAMUS

Upon the earth there is not his like.
—Job XL–XLI

Gurgling, splashing, drifting, floating, wallowing
in that murky element in which he holds sway,
the hippo is not frightened by a turbulent eddy.
He breaches like a mammoth whale or, bobbing,
makes a dark bristly archipelago slowly moving
just under the water's filmy surface complacency.
On land, he eats grass like an ox or a donkey.
Behold his strong limbs like thick bars of iron!
His massive bones are heavy tubes of bronze.
Although he's barely shaded by tall lotus trees
or by a waving cover of spongy, hollow rushes,
under the brook's yellow willows he lies prone.
He's fearless in the covert of shimmering reeds,
in the musky secrecy of the sodden black marsh.

The lid of an OLD CIRCUS TRUNK, which was lined with a Zoological Institute broadside. Courtesy of the collections of the Somers Historical Society.

NIGHT WALK

Owls, raccoons, opossums guide us
Over inky trails in the black moat

Of our slow jump to the next stand.
We track dark rails that map the mud.

We don't make camp. We don't eat.
We can't risk the curious or the free.

Something howls. Dry twigs crackle.
Alert for fisty towners who like a clem,

We strain to define every gray shape
Losing its shape in this cloudy soup.

At the clattering lot of a new town, soon
Sleep will come in the calliope of morning.

And stray stars will cling like ornaments
Over the whitening tops of distant trees.

LEATHER-BOUND ROUTE BOOKS from 1839 and 1840. *Courtesy of the collections of the Somers Historical Society.*

• •

THE PHILADELPHIA AND BALTIMORE units of the Zoological Institute published the first known route books in 1835. Route books were produced at the end of the touring season and given to traveling menagerie employees as souvenirs. A permanent record of the season on the road, route books listed the towns visited by the menagerie, the miles driven, the hotels stayed in, the roster of personnel and the highlights of various engagements.

ROUTE BOOK

From Troy to Utica to Rome,
Rome to Syracuse to Ithaca,
Ithaca to Geneva to Attica,
you ask yourself who you are,
and all you ever really know
between the gold coin moon
and the wrinkled sheets of road
is how the route always leads
home—without maps, magnetic
needles of a clock-shaped compass,
or the polestar winking in the dark—
always home, something warm
carried like a coal in a pocket,
not an address that grounds you
to one time and place in space,
but dust in the eyes, mouth, lap
you cannot cough out or do not want to,
a moment that is beyond words,
the precise instant when fear
lifts suddenly like birds flushed
from hidden nests into the harbor
of the clear, cold, startling air.

In Search of History

Where are your yellowed receipts,
your passports, your torn hotel bills,
letters, bills of sale, ticket stubs?

Where are thin, wasp-nest pages
of ledgers, brown ink-spotted diaries?

Who lined steamer trunks or drawers
with your crumbly posters and handbills
calling us, calling us, calling us in?

Or safely stowed those small,
square, cerise and loden books of maps
sending us away or telling us where to go?

How did all your animals live in snow?
What did wives, daughters, sisters do?

Who built your vanished wagons, cages,
theater box seats, those awkward barns?

Who sewed costumes, tents, or trappings
and sewed up contracts, mergers, deals?

Who watched? Wondered? Looked away?

Whose wings, whose hump, whose spiral
horns or shiny black hooves now mingle
beside their trainers, keepers, owners?

Who remembers all your human names—
Early   Frost   Light   Brown   Green   Finch
Quick   Crane—now merged and lowercased
into this one whole, this land, this terrain?

Who hears as I try to speak, to speak
while I balance over that river made of
what we know and what we do not know?

A MAP OF SOMERS, 1867, from an F.W. Beers atlas. Courtesy of the collections of the Somers Historical Society.

CRADLE

There, in the greeny scalene triangle
fifty miles north of a city—sky-
line, bridgespan, rust stain,
mudbank, waterlily
New York—

    in the ancient home of the Kitchawanks,
old Dutch manor of Stephanus Van Cortlandt—
    shard, sword, brick, kiln, plow, black flint—

what cartography cannot contain,
what demographics do not detail,
what history fails to highlight:

    the extraordinary pulsing like a fifth element
    in soil and sycamore.

The names have been changed to name
    this thirty-three-square-mile hamlet:
Amapaugh for "freshwater fish";
Stephentown for Stephen, son of landowner Stephanus;
    Somers for brass-buttoned, broken-ring,
nineteenth-century naval hero Richard Somers;
    cradle for nurture, genesis—
(*cradel, cradol, kratto, grantha*
    meaning *basket, knot*)—

cradle as place of origin, framework,
        tool for harvesting grain or panning gold,
the act of supporting protectively,

        of sheltering or rearing,
an infant's first rocky narrow bed,
the earliest period of life.

From gneiss, granite, loam, red sandstone, and clay,
        to glacial debris (Cobbling Rock
                deposited like a giant red jewel)
to the buried wealth claimed by Clover Hill Mine,

to the bracelet of reservoirs brimming
        and the product of a "never-failing
spring of the purest cold water" sold
in glass bottles by the Granite Springs Water Company
                (hear the thrum and splash
of gristmills, cider mills, paper mills, sawmills, mills
        for carding, fulling, dyeing flax and wool),

to the airy hills "thickly covered
with a growth of oak, hickory, ash, and chestnut"
                among which inclines
                        the ascending, winding smoke
of what cannot be forgotten or captured intact,

to the blood-red fire of passion
kept alive by tales and stories:
                        vision, action, reaction.

This sanctuary, this haven, this refuge
                    will shelter them, support them, hold them
      as those who are yet unnamed come
          from the east, the west, the north, the south
     to be named, to gather this elemental, glittering thread
          now floating
                  in its amniotic bed.

The GRAND FINALE, an 1872 print created by Strobridge Lithographing Company. Popular Graphic Arts Collection, Prints & Photographs Division, Library of Congress, LC-USZ62-1171.

Epilogue

If any group may be said to have shaped the American circus into its traditional form, it is these showmen from Westchester and Putnam Counties. They imported the rare animals, hired the Van Amburghs and the Driesbachs [renowned wild animal trainers], *combined the circus and menagerie and heralded the great elephant heroes. They introduced the posters and couriers of modern advertising, and with them the effusive language that is still part of the entertainment business. It was their wagon shows that created the circus season; and in their visits to the towns and hamlets they educated an audience for the circus that still exists today.*

—*Stuart Thayer, from* Annals of the American Circus, 1830–1847, *Volume II*

The Birth

By Mabel Addis

I was born in Mount Vernon, just about six blocks away from the estate of James McGinnis Bailey of Barnum and Bailey Circus fame. I spent my summers in North Salem, where I heard all about the June house and the cemetery where so many circus families were buried, saw the Close house where Amzi kept his monkeys and shopped in Finney's meat market right by George F. Bailey's old tavern. From there I moved to a farm in Sodom, north of Brewster. School buses were unknown in those days. We walked five miles a day, but it was a fun walk! The road passed by an estate called Stonehenge, where the early circus man "Uncle Nate" Howes once lived; the home of "Clem" the bear, where Tom Thumb frequently visited; "Monkeytown," with its huge old barns that once housed the circus simians. My teenage winter days were spent skating on Vreeland's pond right next to the castle of a famous circus man, Seth B. Howes. How many times when homeward bound we crossed the lawn and tried to peek under the tightly drawn shades to see the mysterious interior of a circus castle! Eventually, I married into a family where one aunt was the daughter of a well-known circus horseman and one great-grandfather had signed the document of the Zoological Institute. Finally, I moved to Somers, met Mrs. Oliver and was *completely* converted to menagerie madness!

MENAGERIE MADNESS

Folklore abounds, but fact eludes the writer who would re-create the story of Hachaliah Bailey. Yet this we do know—it was the year 1775 in that part of the Van Cortlandt Manor known as Hanover (and later as Stephen Town) that a child was born who was to exemplify the American ideals of initiative, enterprise and business acumen. Within his lifetime, these qualities would enable him to develop an institution that would bring joy to the succeeding generations of both the young and young-at-heart: the American circus. His name was Hachaliah Bailey, the son of James and Ann Brown Bailey. His childhood home was a farmhouse overlooking the turnpike that led to the port of Sing Sing on the Hudson River. Hachaliah grew up working with animals on the farm and in time joined many of the men in the area who had found another profitable occupation in addition to their farming. They had become drovers. This work entailed traveling upstate or over into New England to purchase cattle and driving them home to the farms to be readied for market in New York City. It was not only a lucrative business but also a logical one for this area, since the market was approximately a day's journey by foot and sloop to New York City.

If we can assume that Hachaliah Bailey was in the cattle business at the age of twenty-one, then certainly he must have frequented the Bull's Head Tavern with its adjoining cattle yards—a fixture on the Bowery of New York City. This was the headquarters of the drovers and cattle dealers, as well as the source of the latest shipping and market news. If Hachaliah did visit the tavern in 1796, he certainly was aware that the first elephant to be brought to our shores arrived here on April 13 of that year. She was brought here from India by Captain Jacob Crowninshield on his vessel, the *America*. This information was recorded in the ship's log and reported in the newspaper the *New York Argus*. Supposedly, a Welshman named Owen purchased her for the enormous sum of $10,000 and for several years toured the Atlantic seaboard. These facts, if true, present a "history mystery" for the archives of Somers. Namely, since Hachaliah Bailey had a brother-in-law and close business associate named Owen, could this pachyderm eventually have become "Old Bet"? It is known that she was shown in York, Pennsylvania, in 1796; Charleston, South Carolina, in 1797; Philadelphia in 1806; and sometime later passed into complete oblivion.

The more popular version of Hachaliah's acquisition of the pachyderm pet is that a sea captain brother of his bought an African elephant for $20 at a London auction and sold her to Hachaliah for $1,000 in 1815.

The story continues with the new owner's loading the beast on his sloop and sailing up the Hudson to Sing Sing. The long, arduous walk along the turnpike to Somers literally became a forerunner of a Ringling Brothers triumphal entry! Every water stop, and there were many, brought more curiosity seekers to view this eccentric character leading a very strange beast not native to our shores. Why did he purchase so strange a pet? Some sources say that it was to clear the rocky terrain of his farm; others, that he intended to have a show animal from the outset.

It is important to state that the date of the aforesaid transaction is erroneous, the existence of a Bailey brother as a sea captain is questionable and the description of the walk and its influence on the motive for purchase may be purely folklore. Of one fact we are certain. Sometime *before* 1808, Hachaliah Bailey did acquire an elephant. On file in the archives of the Somers Historical Society are three original documents, two of which prove beyond a doubt the ownership of one pachyderm. Their text follows:

> *Articles of Agreement between Hachaliah Bailey of the first part and Andrew Brunn and Benjamin Lent of the second part: The said Brunn and Lent agree to pay said Bailey twelve hundred dollars each for the equal two-thirds of the use of the elephant for one year from the first day of the month. Bailey on his part furnishes one-third of the expenses, and Brunn and Lent the other two-thirds. August 13th, 1808.*

The second document, dated December 9, 1809, while it does not concern Hachaliah immediately, explains the third. Cyrus A. Cady and John E. Russell sell Nero, the Royal Tiger, and cage for

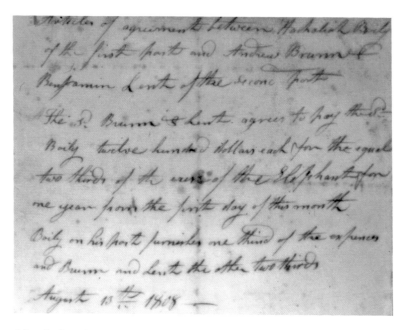

A handwritten lease agreement, dated August 13, 1808, between Hachaliah
Bailey and fellow Somers drovers Andrew Brunn and Benjamin Lent. Bailey
leased two-thirds of the use of "the elephant" to his partners, each of whom paid
$1,200. *Courtesy of the collections of the Somers Historical Society.*

$100 to Benjamin Lent. Four days later, on December 13, 1809,
Hachaliah Bailey hires one-quarter of earnings of an elephant for
the purchase of one-half of Lent's tiger.

An analysis of the first of these documents, in addition to proving
that Hachaliah owned an elephant, would indicate that he must
have had it long enough to determine that taking the animal on
tour was a lucrative business. Otherwise, why would Lent have
wanted to hire her? The second two documents would suggest that
Hachaliah, while relieving himself of some of the tedious travel,
was also enlarging his collection.

In the years that followed, unfortunately, we have no firsthand
description of the Bailey menagerie, its exact content or mode
of travel and display. It is assumed, of course, that Hachaliah,
the current investor or the hired help traveled by night to avoid
"freeloaders" and exhibited the animals in rented barns by day. In

his article "The Crowninshield Elephant," George P. Goodwin of the Museum of Natural History described the Bailey menagerie as consisting of "four wagons, a trained dog, several pigs, a horse, and an elephant." Benjamin Brown, a young Bailey cousin who once took the show on tour, definitely mentioned a lion. Other sources have listed bears. Regardless of the number of animals he displayed, the fact remains that Hachaliah Bailey was the catalyst that gave birth to the American menagerie. Since the itinerary of the Bailey menagerie was quite extensive, covering northern Westchester County, Putnam, Dutchess and parts of New England, there was occasion for many amusing incidents to happen. One favorite supposedly took place in North Salem but could be applied to any town on the route. A group of youngsters, determined to see Old Bet free of charge, spread a trail of potato peelings (her favorite snack) from the highway to a far corner of a field. When Bet took the edible detour, the youth came out of hiding and, with the help of a prepared bonfire, saw the elephant without charge!

The best-known bit of folklore quoted in *The Life of P.T. Barnum* recalls the failure of a certain equal partner to remit to Hachaliah

"Old Bet's Parade," acrylic on canvas, by Somers artist Oscar J. Denny (1919–1995). *Courtesy of the collections of the Somers Historical Society.*

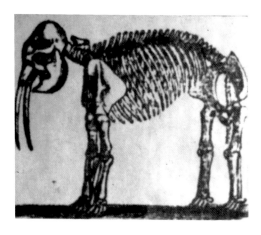

This picture is from a newspaper notice from the *New York Post*, April 18, 1817, about the exhibition of Old Bet's skeleton at 301 Broadway in New York City. *Courtesy of the collections of the Somers Historical Society.*

Bailey his share of the profits. Mr. Bailey arrived at the barn and stood poised with a shotgun aimed at Old Bet. A terrified partner begged him not to shoot. "I only intend to shoot my half of the elephant," said Hachaliah. The partner paid!

Supposedly, about 1815, Hachaliah leased an interest in his menagerie to Nathan Howes of Southeast. As was to be expected, menagerie fever had spread rapidly from Somers to North Salem to Southeast in Putnam County.

In 1816, while on tour near Alfred, Maine, on the way to Berwick, Old Bet was shot by an angry farmer named Donald Davis. He supposedly felt that it was sinful for poor people to be spending their hard-earned cash to see a wicked beast! The names of Hachaliah Bailey and the George Brown Company appear as complainants in the arrest of this man for "trespass." The man apparently was released on bail two days later, and his punishment is not known. The name of Nathan Howes, as the manager of the show, is not mentioned in the newspaper account but appears in the story sent to Somers by Mary Carpenter Kelley.

On April 16, 1817, the *New York Evening Post* printed this notice:

> *The skeleton of that unfortunate Elephant that was shot the 26th of July last, in District of Maine, so well known by the public, is got up for inspection, and may be seen at No. 301 Broadway from Monday the 7th until Wednesday the 30th instant, every day in the week, Sunday excepted, from nine in the morning until*

sunset. The weight of the elephant when it was shot was upward
of 70 hundred pounds. Admission 25 cents.

Ghoulish, perhaps, but practical, and Hachaliah was a businessman.

On October 11, 1816, one Hachaliah Bailey of Somers, in partnership with George Brunn of Boston, commissioned Israel Thorndike to go to Calcutta, India, and for a total of $8,000 to purchase and transport, via the ship *Columbus*, one elephant not more than five feet high. In November 1817, a year later, the ship came back with the elephant, which was named for the ship that transported it. A week earlier, another ship had arrived with an elephant for Hachaliah. This one he promptly named "Little Bet," or "the Learned Elephant." So, two elephants were owned, at least in part, by Hachaliah. Isaac Purdy of North Salem had joined him in the ownership of Columbus with a vested interest of $2,000. By 1832, this elephant had become the property of J.R. and W. Howe with a value of $9,000.

Despite his investment in elephants, Hachaliah must have been contemplating a new venture. In 1820, he began the construction of a large hotel, adding it onto his already-existing two-story brick

This picture is from a notice of an exhibition of Old Bet's hide at P.T. Barnum's American Museum in New York City. *Courtesy of the collections of the Somers Historical Society.*

house at the crossroads. This new building was to be built of brick, sixty feet square and three stories high, with a frame addition containing on its upper floor a large ballroom. The building was completed in 1825 and appropriately named the Elephant Hotel. Now began a vocation for which the owner had been licensed as early as 1803. The hotel was a natural stopover spot for drovers, circus performers, post riders and travelers. High barns to the rear and east housed coaches and animals. The "heavenly-springy" ballroom attracted guests from every direction. Celebrities such as Aaron Burr, Washington Irving, Horace Greeley and Chauncey Depew were among those who would stay here.

By 1827, Hachaliah had erected his famous monument to Old Bet and placed it in front of his hotel—a dressed granite shaft fifteen feet high supported an iron scrollwork on which stood a wooden elephant—appropriately *gilded*! Why not? Certainly she had been worth her weight in gold.

Hachaliah Bailey had embarked on his last Westchester career after an adult life of almost unbelievable activity. During the period of his life's various careers, he had found time to enlist as an adjutant in the New York State Militia, to serve for nine years as postmaster of Somers (1811–20) and to hold the positions of inspector of common schools, overseer of the highway, pound master in charge of stray cattle and toll gate keeper on the newly legislated Croton Turnpike. He was also the owner of the Red Bird and Eagle Stagecoach Line, which traveled from Danbury to New York in winter and in summer connected with the steamer *John Jay* at Sing Sing Landing. In addition, he had managed to become the second-largest landowner in Somers, having amassed 588 acres, some inherited but most purchased. Would you believe that the name *Hachaliah* means "restless, energetic, active"? Is there a doubt?

Hachaliah had spent most of his life in the town of Somers, except for a very brief period when he lived in North Salem. Information about his personal life is vague. From what records we have, he appears to have been married twice—first to Elizabeth Brown and then to Mary Purdy, daughter of Joseph and Letitia Purdy from the town of North Salem. We believe there were eight children, five of whom we know little about, but we have records on Lewis, who was very active in circus business; Joseph, who eventually settled in Maryland; and Calista, who married Enoch Crosby Jr., son of the famous spy. Calista and young Enoch owned the old Union Hotel in Sing Sing, which was eventually purchased by Hachaliah. This is not surprising, for he also owned property in Mount Pleasant, North Salem, Greenburgh and New York City.

Between 1832 and 1836, Hachaliah Bailey was serving Cherry Street and Whitlockville with four-horse post coaches, one to three times weekly, on the Sing Sing–Somers route. With his stagecoach business, his properties and his prospering hotel, it would seem that Hachaliah should have been content for the rest of his life.

On January 14, 1835, menagerie owners and representatives of caravan companies, mostly from this area, got together at the Elephant Hotel and drew up a document to form "one joint stock company for the purpose of exhibiting wild animals belonging to them in company or copartnership for profit." The organization was to be called the Zoological Institute. One hundred and twenty-eight outstanding men signed the document, but Hachaliah's signature was not there. Yet we know he hosted the meeting at his hotel. Two months later, he rented the Elephant Hotel to Isaac Crane of Dutchess County. By 1836, he had sold the business, building and property to Gerard Crane.

That restless, active mind probably was generating a new circus-related project of his own. He was well aware of the fact that Washington, D.C., was a regular stopover for many traveling shows. An early circus showplace was Brown's Amphitheater at 4½ Street near the Capitol. A very popular show at both The Bowery and the Washington Amphitheater featured a number of horses and riders. There was a real need for training and wintering quarters for animals in the Washington area. On December 19, 1837, Hachaliah and Mary Bailey of Westchester purchased from one Randolph the entire Pearson Patent (except for small tracts sold to Lacy and Adams). Hachaliah, wealthy showman, cattleman and hotel proprietor with extensive investments in circus menageries and steamboats, paid $6,000 for 526 acres plus thirty poles! He had acquired the land with an old mansion called Maury (one hundred rooms!) at the crossroads of two main highways (Leesburg Turnpike and Columbia Turnpike) and only three miles from Little River

Turnpike (the main highway to the west). Clever, clever Hachaliah! In the next few years, Lewis and Mariah and their family joined them. On April 18, 1843, Mariah Bailey was deeded the entire estate by her father-in-law. This talented equestrienne became the matriarch of the crossroads for the next fifty years.

Supposedly, while on a visit to Somers, the man who could handle an elephant succumbed to the kick of a vicious horse. He is buried on the Main Street of his birthplace, close by his Elephant Hotel and Old Bet. His tombstone reads:

Hachaliah Bailey
Died September 2, 1845
Aged 70 years
Enterprise
Perseverance
Integrity

OTHER SOMERS SHOWMEN

Benjamin Brown and Joshua Purdy Brown

Menagerie fever spread rapidly in Somers among the relatives and neighbors of Hachaliah Bailey. Benjamin Brown, a young cousin, was hired by Bailey and Finch to take out the elephant and lion. He soon joined Hachaliah's son, Lewis Bailey, and cousin Purdy Brown to tour Ohio, Kentucky and Tennessee. His next venture was with his own menagerie and circus touring the Caribbean. In the 1830s, he became associated with June, Titus and Angevine, joining Stebbins June in a fascinating quest for giraffes in the interior of Africa. The year 1840 found him taking giraffes for the combine to London to work with Isaac Van Amburgh. He returned to Somers with the giraffes, a piano and a charming bride, Mary Cops, daughter of the keeper of the royal menagerie in London.

Joshua Purdy Brown, another Somers cousin, toured extensively with his circus. This differed from a menagerie. Menageries were basically displays of unusual animals. Circuses were equestrian shows performed in a circular area. J. Purdy Brown was one of the first managers to use the canvas tent or pavilion. He certainly was a pioneer when he joined with the Somers Wright brothers to exhibit jointly his circus and their menagerie. He was highly respected in the South for his gentlemanly deportment in the ring and his benevolence in times of disaster.

Lewis Lent

In several instances, a second generation was to be rocked in the cradle of his father and, with the experience of a parent to guide him, was to gain even greater renown. Such was the case with Lewis B. Lent. Born in Somers in 1813, he grew up with his father's small menagerie and soon became familiar with the routine of exhibiting, purchasing and selling animals. By the age of twenty-one, his early experience enabled Lewis to secure a position as an agent for the well-established North Salem company of June, Titus and Angevine. He soon acquired an interest in J.R. and W. Howe's Menagerie and a four-year partnership in Brown and Lent's Circus. This latter show traveled on the Ohio and Mississippi by steamboat. In the 1840s, he was a partner in Van Amburgh's menagerie for a time, visited England with the Sands and Lent Circus and then allied himself with General Rufus Welch. His long association with Welch was dropped for a year while Lewis traveled with Barnum's Tom Thumb and ten elephants. From 1857 to his retirement in 1882, Lewis B. Lent continuously took out shows as an owner or manager. His death in New York City on May 26, 1887, returned to his cradle in Somers a local boy who had achieved fame as "the best agent" of his time.

The Wright Brothers

Micajah Wright kept an inn on the Somers Plain. Situated as he was on the main stream that show business traveled, he could hardly hope to keep his three sons from catching menagerie fever. Only too soon they became involved. Daniel traveled west with a show, fell in love with the area and settled in Ohio. Charles became a proprietor in the prevailing show business of our area and traveled extensively with his younger brother, James. It so happened that in the year 1828, they were exhibiting their menagerie in Charleston, South Carolina, at the same time that J. Purdy Brown was there with his circus. When Brown left Charleston, the Wrights followed, and they exhibited together several times successfully. This marked the first traveling combination of a menagerie and circus, according to historian Stuart Thayer. When Charles returned to Somers, he married Elizabeth Maria Smith, who consented to be his bride only if he stayed home. Charles became a farmer and eventually bought the old Bailey homestead where Hachaliah had been born. James remained in the South, where he became a planter, banker and merchant. Interestingly enough, however, Charles did not abandon show business. A number of letters in the Somers Historical Society's archives indicate that he was buying, selling and arranging show routes and investing in circus ventures while keeping his word to his spouse by staying on the farm.

The Crane Brothers

Thaddeus and Gerard Crane came to Somers from the neighboring town of North Salem in 1822 and purchased considerable property from the Brown estate. Both brothers were very much involved with that "peculiar calling" known as the menagerie business. To give you an idea of the extent of their involvement, consider this extract from a bill of sale:

> State of Virginia of Northampton County, and State of Pennsylvania do this day Bargain, Sell and Deliver unto Thaddeus and Gerard Crane of Westchester County, New York, a Brazilian tiger and tigress, an African leopard and leopardess, two English organs, a bass drum, an Italian cymbal, two monkeys, the Cotamunda, two wagons and five horses with

harness, together with the signs, cuts, and all the apparatus that belongs to said operation of animals—for the consideration of three thousand five hundred dollars.

On March 15, 1825, a bill of sale from Marcus Sloat of Carmel conveyed to the Crane brothers one equal and undivided third part of an elephant called "Pet" for $3,000.

In addition to being an early showman, Gerard was an active partner in the powerful North Salem combine of June, Titus, Angevine and Crane, as well as a town of Somers supervisor, a banker and an entrepreneur. He built his famous and impressive Stone House in 1849, with its long hip-roofed animal house for wintering show animals. It was from here that his famous rhinoceros, which normally required eight horses to pull him from town to town, once escaped for a half-mile stroll down the highway—by himself.

APPENDIX B

The Circus from Menagerie to Mud Show

By Dr. John S. Still

Nearly 130 individuals who were engaged in the menagerie business assembled on January 14, 1835, and drew up and signed a historic document: *The Articles of Association of the Zoological Institute*. Surely, this was the birth certificate for the American circus business. Who were these history makers who organized for the purpose of "keeping a large collection of rare and curious animals, and exhibiting them for the *joint benefit, interest and advantages* of the owners…by means of which the *knowledge of natural history* may be more generally diffused and promoted and rational curiosity gratified"? We know their names but not much about their appearances, except for Gerard Crane, whose portrait hangs in the Somers Historical Society, Rufus Welch and perhaps a few others. We might wonder about their thoughts as they waited for the proceedings to get underway. Did they think back over the previous quarter of a century and the uncoordinated activities that eventually brought about this meeting? Or were they practical-minded businessmen concerned primarily with the present and the future and with ensuring their financial success through cooperation? Undoubtedly the latter because that was the business at hand. A little daydreaming, however, would have reminded them of those who had gone before. There were the equestrians, for example, the acrobats and tumblers and the clowns. Even before they appeared, though, wild or exotic animals were being exhibited, one or two at a time, in tavern yards, barns or wherever the owner could charge admission. Perhaps more common than creatures from far-off lands were the occasional trained bear and, especially, educated dogs, ponies and now and then a monkey. Can you imagine the reaction to seeing an elephant for the first time—perhaps fascination, consternation, disbelief? All of these, no doubt, for this was the largest creature to set foot in the Western Hemisphere since prehistoric times. Small wonder that people were willing to pay money just to gawk at one. When elephants were taught to perform various tricks, they were even more popular. They became the mainstay of any circus program.

Meanwhile, in 1793, about the time the first elephant was brought to the United States, another immigrant made history in his own right. He was John Bill Ricketts, a Scotsman recently arrived in Philadelphia from London, and he was an accomplished equestrian. Bareback performers were already appearing in this country, but Ricketts was not only the best of his day, he also was the first to present a true circus program by combining the talents of the equestrian with those of a clown, an acrobat and a ropewalker all in one show. The only ingredient still lacking was the menagerie, and it remained for New Yorkers to add that element twenty-five years or so later. Ricketts was a favorite of President George Washington, who attended his circus at least twice. He also sold Ricketts his famous Revolutionary War horse, Jack, then twenty-eight years old. It may have made the president feel like a shrewd bargainer, but Ricketts's eye for publicity was not surpassed even by P.T. Barnum himself a couple generations later.

What was called a "circus" in those years was a building—usually a temporary structure with an amphitheater and no roof. As time passed, some more permanent buildings were erected. Ricketts built not only the one in Philadelphia but also eventually others in New York City, Albany and elsewhere. A rare insight into the operation of this famous circus company is provided in a memoir written by John Durang, a theatrical performer who became one of Ricketts's stars as a ropewalker, dancer, acrobat and leaper. One of his interesting accounts describes the troupe's five-day journey by sloop up the Hudson River from New York to Albany in 1797 and its three-week stay before moving on to Montreal. The personnel consisted of Ricketts, Durang, a musician, a groom, an assistant and Master Hutchins (a young boy apprentice), plus six performing horses. Often, a clown would be included. The arrival of this first circus troupe ever to visit Albany aroused much interest and curiosity. Ricketts obtained permission from the corporation to perform, and the first week was devoted to erecting the "circus," a temporary structure consisting of the boxes, elevated with a roof; the pit, with seats open and low; a movable stage to dance on; a dressing room; an orchestra; a stable; and a fence around the ring. The first performance, on July 31, took in $160, but Durang noted that "there was about twice the number of people out side of the building some boreing holes thro' the board to get a peep." He found the people unsociable and the town dull. Most of the women, married or single, went barefoot, and the broken English they spoke (being descended from Hollanders) made the girls in particular nearly impossible to understand. The women, he commented,

> *are in general homely and frightened when a stranger speaks to them, but time will reform and accomplish them...I have seen more cripples and blind people in this town than any other I have been in. The sturgeon fish is a preculiar* [sic] *usual dish in this town, known by the name of Albany beef. I have seen the skins lay in the streets and the hogs feed on them.*

On the night of August 5, a disastrous fire broke out, threatening the stable. The troupe managed to save the horses by herding them into the ring of the circus, after which they pitched in and helped the citizens carry their property from their burning homes. In four hours, Durang wrote, 230 buildings were destroyed. Subsequently, a benefit performance held for the aid of the homeless attracted a full house. As was customary, other days' shows were designated benefits for various performers. Durang received $100 from his benefit. Business suffered in general, however, from the fire, so the company packed up and set out for Montreal on August 14. Ricketts, incidentally, continued to earn the admiration and praise of spectators and writers alike. Disaster, however, plagued him. Fire consumed his buildings in New York and Philadelphia, an ill-fated voyage to the West Indies resulted in his being captured by pirates and his horses sold and in 1800 the ship on which he was bound for England was lost at sea. The last performance by America's first great rider and its first circus impresario had taken place in Philadelphia on April 23, 1800.

Hindsight suggests that this was, in a sense, a turning point in the development of the circus. Ricketts's death did not bring about a decline in the popularity or prowess of equestrian entertainers, to be sure, but the pendulum was about to start swinging in the direction of the menagerie. The impetus would come from Somers, and the man responsible for it was Hachaliah Bailey. For nearly a century, adventurous sailors had been bringing back from Europe or Africa an occasional lion, leopard, camel or other strange creature to appeal to the curiosity of their fellow Americans. Advertisements appeared as early as 1728 for a lion in New York, a camel in 1739 and so on. Finally, in 1796, a newspaper reported that the ship *America* had brought home from Bengal an ELEPHANT in perfect health, the first ever seen in America. It was said to have cost $10,000. The elephant was claimed to possess

> the adroitness of the beaver, the intelligence of the ape, and the fidelity of the dog. He [it was actually a female] is the largest of quadrupeds; the earth trembles under his feet. He has the power of tearing up the largest trees and yet is tractable to those who use him well.

The awesome-sounding leviathan was in reality two years old and stood six feet, four inches tall!

For about a decade "The Elephant" (she was apparently never given a name) had America to herself, but then came Old Bet. According to tradition, she was imported by a ship's captain who sold her to his brother, Hachaliah Bailey of Somers, for $1,000. Stuart Thayer, however, has identified the artist Edward Savage as Old Bet's original owner in America in 1804, before Mr. Bailey came into her life two or three years later. Her arrival at Somers was long thought to have occurred about 1815, but among the treasures in the manuscript collections of the Somers Historical Society are two agreements that place her there at least seven years earlier. On August 13, 1808, Andrew Brown and Benjamin Lent agreed to pay Hachaliah Bailey $1,200 each "for the equal two-thirds of the use of the Elephant for one year." Expenses would be shared according to the same ratio. The following year, Bailey rented to Lent one-fourth of the use of earnings of "a certain Beast or Animal called an Elephant," in exchange for which he was paid half of the "Royal Tiger" that Lent had bought for $1,000 a few days earlier. The interest in seeing Old Bet was so great that Bailey or a partner traveled with her not only around the countryside in New York State but also eventually through Connecticut and most of New England. After several years on the road, she met a violent death in far-off Maine, shot, as the *Poughkeepsie Journal* put it, "by some unknown wretch" on July 26, 1816. Rumor blamed the incident variously on superstition, resentment over the money leaving the locality and charges that Old Bet frightened unsuspecting horses. The prosperity that she had generated—both directly and through Hachaliah Bailey's expansion of his business by buying other imported animals—produced a famous memorial to her, the Elephant Hotel, and a statue on a column.

An even more far-reaching legacy could be found in the proliferation of traveling menageries operated by Bailey's neighbors and acquaintances in and around Somers and from various places in Westchester, Putnam and Dutchess Counties. Circus history as we know it today would not have been written without such names as Gerard and Thaddeus Crane; Lewis Titus; John June; Caleb Angevine; Aaron Turner; Seth B. Howes; Rufus Welch; James Raymond; Hiram Waring; J.R., Epenetus and William Howe; Lewis Lent; Zebedee Macomber; Darius Ogden; Eisenhart Purdy; Charles Wright; and Richard Sands, to mention only some of the more familiar names. Their imagination, perseverance, determination and willingness to gamble inspired them not only to risk their money and property to organize and operate menageries, caravans, zoological institutes and whatever else they were called but also to carry on an international trade in wild animals; some even went to Africa actively collecting specimens. Incidentally, as far as the name was concerned, the word "circus" was assiduously avoided because of the unsavory connotation attached to it in many circles. This situation continued for many years. At a small college in Ohio, for example, the rules of conduct for students in the school year 1864–65 included proper attention to good morals by abstaining from intoxicating drink and by not engaging in games of chance, using profane or indecent language, carrying firearms, visiting circuses or theaters or other immoral conduct. By the early 1830s, large companies boasting several dozen animals, reptiles, a band and horses and wagons were fanning out through the Northeast, and some were even reaching the Midwest and South.

An interesting glimpse of the variety and value of menagerie livestock is provided by a manuscript entitled "An Estimation of J.R. and W. Howe & Co. Exhibition, November 21, 1834." The two highest-priced animals were a rhinoceros valued at $10,000 and the elephant Columbus at $9,000. A Bactrian camel was listed at $3,000; a white bear at $2,750; and a zebra, a gnu and two tigers at $2,000 each, after which the values dropped sharply to $400 and below. Interestingly enough, the show did not have a lion at that time. The total value of the menagerie, including seventeen cages and wagons, was $46,583. Another historic document at the Somers Historical Society is a broadside advertising the auction of animals, horses, etc., to be held at the Elephant Hotel on August 22 and 23, 1837. All the property and effects of the eastern section of the Zoological Institute, the circus traveling with it and another menagerie unit situated at Somers were to be sold. Included were the elephants Virginius and Siam, a female rhinoceros, lions, tigers, camels, leopards and many others. The two-and-a-half-year-old Zoological Institute was feeling the effect of the widespread depression in 1837.

These were some of the enterprises headed by the men who assembled here on January 14, 1835. In addition to their partnership and their collective efforts in organizing the Zoological Institute, some of them earned recognition for special feats or ideas. Most of these were "firsts" in circus history, and nearly all occurred in New York. For example, the circus tent evolved gradually, starting with a canvas enclosure around a stable yard and eventually placing a covering over it. New Yorkers imported the first giraffe (which some called a "camelopard") and the first rhinoceros (also called a "unicorn"), and they borrowed from English designs to build some of the fanciest bandwagons. James W. Bancker, a native of New York and the first American-born circus proprietor, was also the first to advertise his troupe as a circus. "Bancker's New York Circus" opened in Albany on February 27, 1824, combining its performance with that of the Grand Caravan featuring the elephant Tippoo Sultan. This was the first time that individual units of a circus and a menagerie were presented together in the United States.

Some famous "firsts" were circus performers rather than operators. The most historic of these, and certainly the greatest star of the nineteenth century, was the young man from Fishkill with the unlikely name of Isaac Van Amburgh. Born in 1808, he grew up fascinated with the wild animals in itinerant menageries. By the early 1830s, he was working for Raymond & Company as keeper of lions and tigers. His great opportunity came in 1833, when he was permitted to enter the cage and demonstrate his courage

A Currier & Ives lithograph showing Van Amburgh & Co.'s triumphal car passing the Astor House in New York City on April 20, 1846. *Popular Graphic Arts Collection, Prints & Photographs Division, Library of Congress, LC-USZC2-3131.*

and rapport with the jungle cats before an astonished audience. It brought him instant fame and a new career as a featured performer on various shows, two triumphal years in England and Europe where he was lionized by royalty and the public alike and, finally, his own circus. Van Amburgh was unquestionably the best-known name attached to any show in the twenty years preceding his death in 1865. His manager, Hyatt Frost, a native of the town of Southeast, kept the name alive for another thirty years. As a matter of fact, it was sometimes difficult to tell that Van Amburgh himself was not still alive and running the show. Both men were masters of publicity, Van Amburgh especially in his characterization of himself as a Roman gladiator in the lions' den (the subject of a Currier & Ives print) and in the elegant bandwagon he had constructed upon his return from England. Frost was a worthy rival of P.T. Barnum in the lurid, exaggerated prose in his handbills and other printed advertisements in the 1870s and '80s. Consider, for example, the 1885 ad for allegedly the sixty-fifth season, tracing the show's beginnings to 1820 (when Van Amburgh was twelve years old). One of the features of the show was billed as

> *"Quedah"…the rarest animal alive, the offspring of a Mysterious Malay Mountain Mammoth…a descendant of the Prehistoric Monsters that were contemporaneous with the Ichthyosaurus and Pterodactyl. The First Discovered Since the Deluge!*

At the same time that Van Amburgh was becoming the king of the lion tamers (and, incidentally, the first person to put his head in a lion's mouth and live to tell about it), other exciting first-time events were taking place. One that has aroused considerable interest in recent years was the first announced circus street parade. Albany has been a strong contender, based primarily on the front-page advertisement in the *Albany Argus* for May 5, 1837, cited in later secondary sources. Purdy, Welch, Macomber & Co., Proprietors from the Zoological Institute, New York, was coming to town for two days, and it promised to be a spectacular production. Extravagant language vied with dramatic woodcuts trumpeting the praises of, first of all, the Boston Brass Band directed by Edward Kendall, fifteen musicians, twelve on horseback and three riding in the howdah on the elephant's back. The next attraction was Mr. Van Amburgh, who, with a child and a lamb, would at half past two each afternoon enter the cage of six lions, tigers and leopards and combine them into "the most terrific and astonishing groupes [*sic*], forming a sublime and thrilling spectacle." There would also be performances by the elephant and the pony and monkey, plus the "Magnificent Collection of rare Beasts and Birds from Europe, Asia, Africa, and North and South America," including

> *the Unicorn, or one horned Rhinoceros, Polar or White Bear, Eland from Central Africa, Black Ostrich; Kangaroo; Gnu, or Horned Horse; Hindostan, or Great Sloth Bear; Grisly Bears from the Rocky Mountains; Pelicans, Vultures, Hyenas, Zebra, Lama, Camel, Dromedary, Elephant, Buffalo, Leopards, Tigers, Lions, and numerous other rare and interesting animals.*

All for only twenty-five cents' admission. The Boston Brass Band would "precede the Caravans, and take the lead on entering into places of exhibition." It would also announce the arrival of the Grand Cavalcade at the "splendid Pavilion" that would accommodate six thousand people at a time, with seats for the women and children. This information and the cut clearly suggest a street procession. It may well have been, but it wasn't the first. Displayed in the Elephant Hotel is a broadside—a real treasure—promoting J.R. and W. Howe & Co.'s New York Menagerie. After proclaiming the talents of the twelve-member band and the performing elephant Columbus and mentioning the numerous animals in the menagerie, it informs the public that the entire train of horses, wagons, etc., will arrive in town between the hours of eleven and twelve o'clock on Thursday morning. In addition, "the proprietors pledge that they will make a General Parade, with their entire Establishment...It will be headed by the New York Band of Music, and the celebrated Elephant Columbus." The date? September 8, 1834, nearly three years earlier than the Albany claim. Now the question is—were there any still earlier than the Howes?

Adam Forepaugh & Sells Brothers 1896 chromolithograph poster. Forepaugh, a horse dealer, founded his own circus in 1865 and became partners with Ephraim, Lewis and Peter Sells in 1896. *Prints & Photographs Division, Library of Congress, LC-USZC4-2987.*

Another controversy has centered on the first circus to travel by rail. Although the appearance of the circus train on the American landscape in the 1870s heralded a different era than we are talking about today—one in which names such as Ringling, Barnum, Bailey, Forepaugh, Sells, Robinson, Christy and Cole arrived on the scene—the background of the argument is pertinent here. In the first place, despite their size, the shows touring the eastern half of the United States in midcentury were still primarily wagon shows trundling and trudging over dirt roads, combating rain, mud, washed-out bridges and other obstacles. Secondly, the man who attempted to do something about it was another New Yorker, Gilbert R. Spalding. Following in the tradition of his earlier counterparts downstate, "Doc" Spalding was the owner of a drug and sundries store in Albany who became a circus entrepreneur by accident. In 1843, he found himself the owner of a down-on-its-luck circus as part of the settlement for debts owed to him. In the next quarter century, Spalding made contributions to the development of the circus far surpassing the credit he has received. He invented the "quarter-poles," which made it possible to enlarge tents to unprecedented size; he and his partner, Charles J. Rogers, took their show aboard a steamboat and toured the Mississippi, leading to their conceiving the idea of the river showboat (their *Floating Palace* was launched in 1852, followed by two others, the *James Raymond* and the *Banjo*), and in 1856 they announced their "NEW RAILROAD CIRCUS for which they have built nine cars of their own!" They explained in a now-rare pamphlet (a copy of which is owned by the New-York Historical Society) that their objective was "to furnish to their Eastern and Northern Patrons the same degree of Novelty, originality and perfection that Messrs. SPALDING & ROGERS have afforded to the citizens of the South and West, on their three Exhibition Steamers." The cars were built expressly for transporting the people, horses and properties of the company, and they were constructed so that they could be taken daily "from the track to the tent." Although the pamphlet characterized its contents as "concisely mentioning the features of their New Show, without any flourishes or hyperbolical descriptions," no punches were pulled in comparing the advantages of the railroad circus with all of its competitors' drawbacks. In this publication, as well as in a newspaper advertisement for Salem, Massachusetts, on June 25, 1856 (in the collections at the Somers Historical Society), Spalding and Rogers's "restraint" took the form of such comparisons as these in calling attention to "the great and inseparable drawbacks" of the Old Fogy Wagon Shows:

> *No more Skeleton Team Horses, fagged out Ring Horses, tired Performers, sleepy Clowns, dillapadated* [sic] *Harness and Wagons, and tarnished Trappings—the natural consequence of twenty miles a day of night travel over rough roads.*
>
> *Under the old regime, the Company are always fatigued and querulous; the Ring Horses leg-weary, and anything but the flashy animals they are pictured on the bills; the Clown loses his mother wit, if he ever had any, and is too sleepy to nourish any he may have acquired; the performers wade through a dull and vapid performance with the least possible labor; the musicians*

The Grand Lay-Out, an 1874 lithograph by Gibson & Co. showing a circus parade winding around a series of tents. A crowd watches from beside a railroad train. Transporting a circus by rail became more common in the 1860s and 1870s. *Popular Graphic Arts, Prints & Photographs Division, Library of Congress, LC-USZ62-1028.*

scarcely open their eyes until they give the long wished for blast for the afterpiece; the ticket seller gruffly makes the change for the ticket, in receiving which the door-keeper rudely thrusts you aside in his dreamy listlessness; the ushers follow you at a snail's pace while you hunt up a seat for yourself; the landlord works all night to wake up the company to breakfast at three in the morning, and for his pains often has his bill disputed for a few pennies by the worn out manager.

This show was a circus in the old tradition—equestrians, gymnasts and clowns—and apparently carried no menagerie. It did, however, transport horses in railroad cars. The railroad circus also could not travel great distances because of the problem of the different gauges of the tracks from one road to another.

In a story that is marked by new ideas, new attractions and "first-time-ever" accomplishments, it is gratifying to have at least one old standby to furnish continuity and stability to circus history. We have that in a long list of distinguished performers whose names belong in any hall of all-time circus greats. Some we have heard before, but they bear repeating as we ponder what the circus would have been without the likes of Columbus, Hannibal, Tippoo Sultan, Bolivar, Tippoo Saib, Queen Anne, Siam, Romeo and Juliet, Horatio, Virginius, Xerxes, Antony and Cleopatra, Pizarro, Cortez and, of course, Old Bet, the most important of all these historic pachyderms (with due respect to "The Elephant" of the 1790s). Their physical attributes and their ability to learn and perform amazing stunts made elephants everlastingly popular. Often they have been the feature of the circus.

One of the most famous was Columbus, who has ambled in and out of this discourse several times. He was the third elephant in the United States and the first male. After arriving in 1817, he toured independently or with menageries for thirty-four years until he died in 1851 after falling through a bridge at North Adams, Massachusetts. Columbus is featured in a rare broadside in the New York State Museum Collections. The existence of the broadside itself is quite fortuitous in that it was used by Chester Elsworth, a trunk maker in Troy, New York, to line a small trunk now owned by the museum. Columbus was brought by his keeper to Troy in May 1828 for a three-day appearance at Waters' Tavern. The enterprising manager of the Troy Circus, which featured Mr. Stickney, the Celebrated Flying Horseman; Master Burton from Albany; the Celebrated horse Arab; and ground and lofty tumbling, quickly arranged for Columbus to join the presentations of the circus. As a result, Columbus's stay in Troy was extended by another week. The broadside and newspaper advertisements described Columbus as being twenty-five years old, nearly ten feet high and weighing upwards of eight thousand pounds. Among the tricks he could perform were

> to draw a cork from a bottle, drink the contents, and hand the cork and bottle to the keeper; take a lady or gentleman on his trunk and carry them round in perfect safety; it will balance on either of its feet, change from side to side, dance, and keep time correctly to music, answer when spoken to, kneel, lie down, roar at request, &c. &c. It will also raise its keeper on its proboscis and toss him over its head, the keeper alighting on the Elephant's back.

Some of the elephants met tragic deaths, including Queen Anne, whose trainer, according to one account, allowed her to drink a barrel of icy-cold water at Zanesville, Ohio, one cold morning, "and that was the last of Queen Anne." Siam also died at Zanesville from being chilled standing out in heavy rain. When Tippoo Sultan refused to come out of a pond, it is said "several balls were fired into him by way of persuasion, from the effects of which he died." Juliet was the victim of injuries sustained when a bridge collapsed near Johnston, New York; her bones are on exhibit at the Johnstown Historical Society's Museum. Romeo subsequently turned vicious and was reported to have died at "Somerstown," New York, chained to a tree, "from an overdose of pitchfork."

The most famous elephant of all, of course, was Jumbo, whose brief American career ended tragically. He was not only one of Barnum's publicity triumphs, but he was also beloved by the people—especially the children—of America. Although he was not part of the menagerie-to-mud show history, he did indeed

This 1882 lithograph by J.H. Bufford's Sons comes from a sheet music cover. It depicts Jumbo carrying a group of children. *Prints & Photographs Division, Library of Congress, LC-USZ62-38877 DLC.*

carry on the tradition of elephant stardom. He was a creature of the 1880s, but in a sense he marked the end of a historic era. From that time forward, elephants have continued to be given names and proved to be talented performers, but none has won the individual renown enjoyed by some of their nineteenth-century predecessors. From Old Bet to Jumbo, they helped to create an important chapter in our story, and they have brought me to the end of the tale.

Selected Bibliography

Chindahl, George L. *A History of the Circus in America*. Caldwell, ID: Caxton Printers, 1959.

Culhane, John. *The American Circus: An Illustrated History*. New York: Henry Holt & Company, Inc., 1990.

Durant, John, and Alice Durant. *Pictorial History of the American Circus.* New York: A.S. Barnes & Company, Inc., 1957.

Koegel, Otto. *Petition to the Postmaster General of the United States in Support of the Claim that Somers, New York Is the Birthplace of the American Circus*. Somers, NY, 1966.

May, Earl Chapin. *The Circus from Rome to Ringling*. New York: Dover Publications, 1963.

Murray, Marian. *Circus! From Rome to Ringling.* Westport, CT: Greenwood Press, 1973.

Scharf, J. Thomas, ed. *History of Westchester County, New York*. Philadelphia: L.E. Preston & Co., 1886.

Somers: Its People and Places, 1788–1988. Somers, NY: Somers Historical Society, 1989.

Still, John. "The Circus from Menagerie to Mud Show." Circus Symposium. Elephant Hotel, Somers, New York, September 8, 1984.

Thayer, Stuart. *Annals of the American Circus.* Vol. 2, *1830–1846.* Seattle, WA: Peanut Butter Publishing, Inc., 1986.

———. *Annals of the American Circus.* Vol. 3, *1848–1860.* Seattle, WA: Dauven & Thayer, 1992.

———. *Traveling Showmen: The American Circus Before the Civil War.* Detroit, MI: Astley & Ricketts, Ltd., 1997.

WEBSITES

tps.cr.nps.gov
www.circushistory.org
www.somershistoricalsoc.org
www.southeastmuseum.org

About the Contributors

THE SOMERS HISTORICAL SOCIETY was founded in 1956 in Somers, New York, as a not-for-profit educational corporation. Its mission is to promote and encourage historical research, educate others about the history of the community, collect and preserve historical artifacts pertaining to the early history of Somers and environs and act as a steward for historical resources in the local community. The society maintains and curates historical properties in Somers, including the Wright-Reis Homestead; Mount Zion Church, listed on the National Register of Historic Places; and Tomahawk Chapel. The society also exhibits portions of its world-class collection of early nineteenth-century American circus artifacts, as well as other items pertaining to the region, in a small museum located in its offices on the third floor of the Elephant Hotel, a National Historic Landmark. www.somershistoricalsoc.org

On September 8, 1984, a CIRCUS SYMPOSIUM organized by the Somers Historical Society was held at the Elephant Hotel. The symposium commemorated the 150th anniversary of the forming of the Zoological Institute in Somers, New York. The essays in this book have been excerpted from talks delivered by speakers who participated in this symposium.

FLORENCE S. OLIVER (1915–2011) was curator of the Somers Historical Society Museum from 1968 to 1975 and subsequently served as the town historian from 1975 until her death in May 2011. She worked ceaselessly to keep Somers history alive and was the driving force behind securing National Historic Landmark status for the Elephant Hotel, the seventeenth such national landmark in Westchester County.

MABEL ADDIS (1919–2004) began her teaching career in a one-room school in Brewster, New York. She served as president of the Somers Historical Society from 1981 to 1984 and was the coauthor of *Brewster Through the Years*; *Katonah: A History of a New York Village*; *History of Southeast*; and *Somers: Its People and Places.*

DR. JOHN S. STILL (1922–2003) was curator of Historical Collections at the Ohio Historical Society and chief of the History Curatorial Unit at the New York State Museum in Albany, where he worked from 1967 until his retirement in 1988. Dr. Still also served as New York's acting state historian from 1976 to 1980. His particular interest was the history of popular entertainment, especially the circus.

Old Bet's statue and the Elephant Hotel. *Photograph by Jeff Zimmerman.*

About the Author

Jo Pitkin grew up in Somers, New York. She received a BA in creative writing and literature from Kirkland College, Clinton, New York, and an MFA in poetry from the Writers' Workshop at the University of Iowa. She is the author of *The Measure* (Finishing Line Press) and the forthcoming *Commonplace Invasions* collection (Salmon Poetry). Her award-winning poems have appeared in such journals and anthologies as *Little Star, Ironwood, Quarterly West, BigCityLit, Nimrod International Journal, Vanguard Voices of the Hudson Valley, Connecticut River Review, Riverine: An Anthology of Hudson Valley Writers, Stone Canoe: A Journal of Arts and Ideas from Upstate New York* and others. After working as an editor at Houghton Mifflin Company in Boston, Jo pursued a career as a freelance writer for educational publishers throughout the United States and is the credited author of more than forty books for kindergarten through twelfth-grade students. She currently lives in the Hudson River Valley in a former public schoolhouse built in 1830.